All Men Become Brothers

All Men Become Brothers

A Day in the Life of Father Nguyen Van Ly

Koenraad De Wolf

RESOURCE *Publications* • Eugene, Oregon

ALL MEN BECOME BROTHERS
A Day in the Life of Father Nguyen Van Ly

Copyright © 2016 Koenraad De Wolf. All rights reserved. Except for brief quotations in critical publications or reviews, no part of this book may be reproduced in any manner without prior written permission from the publisher. Write: Permissions, Wipf and Stock Publishers, 199 W. 8th Ave., Suite 3, Eugene, OR 97401.

Resource Publications
An Imprint of Wipf and Stock Publishers
199 W. 8th Ave., Suite 3
Eugene, OR 97401

www.wipfandstock.com

PAPERBACK ISBN: 978-1-4982-8952-8
HARDCOVER ISBN: 978-1-4982-8954-2
EBOOK ISBN: 978-1-4982-8953-5

Manufactured in the U.S.A. 05/25/16

Contents

I

Midnight

"I thought Vietnam was a free country?"

The Lieutenant threateningly pushed his revolver under my chin.

"Doesn't Article 3 of the Constitution ensure freedom of religion?" I asked him in a shrill voice.

The man pushed me away. He didn't understand what was happening to him. At the *My Chanh* market roadblock, more and more cyclists were showing up. They almost looked like ghosts in the morning mist to the patrol that guarded the site.

"The curfew. You're violating the curfew," yelled the Lieutenant, who was now gesticulating in all directions. "It lasts until six in the morning."

"If my information is correct, the curfew was lifted two years ago."

"Go back!" he ordered. "Go back to where you came from. Now!"

"Why should we? We are going to venerate Our Lady of La Vang."

Our group of pilgrims responded enthusiastically and spontaneously began singing the *Song of Peace* by Kim Long:

> Lord, teach me to love and serve God.

Make me an instrument of your peace.
Where there is hatred, let me sow love . . .

"Control!" the Lieutenant shouted. "We are going to check everyone's documents! Now!"

"Here is my temporary I.D. card. Your colleagues in the State Security confiscated my I.D. card last month."

"Not valid," he barked. The officer he called to assist him also shook his head.

"But don't you know me? I am Father Ly—a 'good friend' of Pham Van Dong." I gesticulated as if I were the equal of Prime Minister.

My humor really didn't seem to amuse them, and the atmosphere became even dicier when those of us without identity cards were told we would be taken away.

"Who do you think you are?" The lieutenant paced up and down. "Those who do not have an I.D. card, come with me. Now! Immediately!"

I protested. "Do we really need an I.D. for a one day excursion? Which Article of the law did we violate?"

The Lieutenant flashed his revolver, taunting, "I represent the law here!"

"Now it gets really exciting." My neighbor said as he gave a nervous smile.

"I think it's the first time since of Communist takeover in 1975 that something is happening here."

"You're coming with us?"

"Sixty-five kilometers is too far. Next month, I'll be 72 and my legs . . ." he sighed. "But my son and grandson will participate."

"Why won't you try? We'll push you when the way goes uphill. Some participants are even older than you."

He shook his head.

"No, no, no. Though, I hear you still don't have a bike. Here, take mime."

"I can't accept . . ."

"You know, this is a real Peugeot. Do you see clawing lion logo? Indestructible," he boasted. "I bought that iron horse in 1939 with my first savings that I had earned in the Michelin rubber plantation. You can't say no."

My neighbor put the bike in the lobby of the rectory when Father Tran Van Qui entered.

"So early! Mass is at 6:00 p.m. Or do you have an appointment with the communist major?" I continue teasing him. "If you're late, I could say Mass. I've also prepared a sermon."

"You're not allowed to do so," he said surly. "And you know that very well. Anyway, you won't get the opportunity. I'll be back in time."

Van Ly and his neighbor were laughing, while Van Qui looked at the bike with surprise.

"You have a bike?"

"I am going to repair it, tinker with it. It's a service for my neighbor," I lied.

"Don't you have anything better to do?"

I pretended not to hear him and soon Van Qui left the presbytery.

"Fortunately the Vietnamese Catholics still have Our Lady of La Vang. But her name is taboo for the Communists. But tomorrow we will celebrate the feast of the Assumption of Our Lady in a dignified manner."

"Did you request a permission?"

"What do you think? Of course not. The answer would undoubtedly have been 'no.' Even worse, the police would do anything to prevent the pilgrimage."

"But is everyone informed?"

"Not yet. I was extremely carefully. The people I told have been sworn to secrecy, because such is necessary for our undertaking. But I still have an opportunity tonight."

At the end of the Mass, I climbed the pulpit.

"Announcements. Tomorrow, August 15, 1981, is the Feast of the Assumption. We'll venerate Our Lady of La Vang. Meet in the church at three o'clock," I said casually.

Smiles everywhere; only Van Qui and the Communist major looked astonished. But my next announcement about the catechism classes diverted their attention.

"Since when is Mass at three o'clock?" asked Van Qui in the vestry. "It's normally at five o'clock!"

"Did I say three o'clock?" I could barely hide my amusement.

In the silence of the middle of the night, cyclists showed up from all over.

"What do you think, sister?"

"The grapevine had done its work."

I saw radiant faces everywhere.

"Look, those people have brought lanterns," whispered Tri Hieu. "They will come in handy."

"Will you carry the red lantern at the rear?" I asked.

"Only arrived yesterday," she smiled, "and already ordered to work."

Shortly after 3:00 a.m., I signaled with my arm, and the long column started moving in silence. Once over the hill, people burst out laughing.

"What a performance to quietly slip away," Ms. Hieu said proudly. "You're awfully brave!"

"Now we only have to reach La Vang. I will keep a steady tempo. The pace should not be too rapid because everyone at the back must be able to follow."

When the road goes uphill, I asked the young people to help the older pilgrims. At the top of a hill I inspected "my troops."

"About two hundred participants! All expectations are exceeded."

I looked at my sister when the last people crossed the top. "Ah! To breathe in free air!" The adrenaline raced through my body.

A minivan arrived in a big cloud of dust. Eight nuns of the Order of the Holy Cross hadn't been allowed to continue their journey. They were stopped at the *My Chanh* roadblock, and the driver was interrogated.

"Papers!"

The driver gave them to the Lieutenant.

"Look here!" the Lieutenant barked. "What's written here? You are only allowed to transport six passengers. And that's not all, your license is only valid as far as the boundary of Hue Station."

"I have . . . the nuns . . ." the man stammered.

"Back!" the Lieutenant shouted. "Go back immediately! And tomorrow you can search for another job. Your driver's license is hereby revoked."

The driver and the nuns turned round, but I didn't want to be pushed around. I put on my cassock, and I told everyone to be quiet. "Friends, let us pray together. If they don't let us through this afternoon, we will go on praying until the evening and, if need be, all night."

When I kneeled, everyone followed my example. I took my *Pater Noster.*

"Hail Mary, full of grace, the Lord is with thee, blessed art thou among women, and blessed is the fruit of thy womb, Jesus."

"Holy Mary, Mother of God, pray for us sinners now and at the hour of our death. Amen."

As more pilgrims arrived in *My Chanh*, the prayers grew louder. I was beaming when my colleague, Phan Van Loi, reinforced our troops with his own group.

"I.D. cards," shouted the lieutenant once again. "I want everyone's I.D. card!"

Meanwhile the agents started to panic.

"What are we going to do with the pile of these cards?"

"There is no end to this work." He let out a deep sigh. The man felt more and more uncomfortable. Hundreds of people from *My Chanh* and the surrounding villages and hamlets gathered around the market.

"I don't feel good about this," an agent said. "Don't you sense a threat emanating from that repetitive prayer and that silent mass of bystanders?"

Suddenly the District Captain of the State Security arrived in a limousine. He was a war veteran and only had one arm.

"Oh, Father Ly, is that you? What a surprise to see you here?" he said in a friendly voice.

"This is something other than your daily visit to *Doc So*."

"Traveling without a permit. That is a serious offense. And you know that," he said sternly.

"A permit? What permit? Vietnam is a free country, right?"

"Don't take me for a ride," he warned. But when the captain looked at the group of people, he didn't want any further difficulties.

"Comrades," he ordered, "give Father Ly his identity card back."

This was the opportunity I was looking for. I clenched my fists. "It is not enough that you give me back my identity card. Everyone's papers should be returned, and you should allow us to continue our journey."

The Captain consulted the Lieutenant for a long time. "Yes, you may continue your journey, but on foot. Don't use your bikes. Agreement?"

People began to applaud spontaneously. The first pilgrims that got their identity cards back started walking. But Ms. Hieu got on her bike and started to pedal.

"The distance to La Vang is after all twenty kilometers."

"I will get you!"

All the others pilgrims followed that example.

"This looks like a bicycle race, brother."

Everyone was thoroughly enjoying the little bit of freedom that had been won and was delighted upon arrival.

"Look over there," I cried. The large mushroom-shaped steeples were still standing beneath the glittering statue of Our Lady.

I let my tears flow freely and hugged Van Loi.

Three weeks later, Van Loi had starred in a parody of that pilgrimage.

He came on the scene with his bicycle. There was a little boy sitting on a chair behind him. In the middle stood roadblocks. Two policemen and an officer kept him standing.

"Stop!"

"What's going on?" asked Van Loi.

The officer gave a sign to his policemen to take their gun. "I'm the one who's asking the questions. Where you're going to?"

"La Vang."

"What for?"

"To dedicate my nephew to Our Lady. So he'll become a priest."

"That'll be forbidden by law very soon," reacted the officer.

"I don't understand."

"In the future no priests will be ordained."

"That's the first I've heard about it," Van Loi replied.

The officer took confidently took out his revolver, saying, "The study of Marxism-Leninism will, from now on, play a central role in all education programs. And only dedicated communists will be allowed to study religion." The man laughed. "But that will be rare."

"Why?"

"All the truth lies within the Communist ideology," said the officer proudly.

The audience started laughing.

"There's no life, no hope, and no future without communism," continued the man. "But what we need, are good examples—what you Catholic people would call 'holy.' We need 'holy communists' who give an example."

"Mom always said that that I'm giving an example with all my life.'

"So you're a holy man!"

Van Loi looked surprised. "I don't know . . ."

"We need people like you. Come to strengthen our ranks!"

"What must I do?"

"Serve the party and government loyally. No questions. No critical points of view. Just execute what our man of light and leading asks."

"And what'll I get in return?"

"All kinds of profits. You can choose . . . And the higher you get promoted, the more advantages you'll receive."

"Really?"

The officer beamed and put his revolver back in his pocket. "I can feel it; you'll become a holy communist."

Van Loi got on his knees. "Master, can I get your blessing?"

"I'm so glad that at least one Catholic is starting to see the true light behind the red star on the Vietnamese flag."

Again, the audience burst out in laughter and applauded.

"Master, am I, as your humble servant, allowed to make a proposal?"

The officer directed his revolver again on Van Loi's head, "You are, my loyal son."

"Why shouldn't we replace the statue of Our Lady of La Vang by a statue of Marx or Lenin?"

A shiver went through the hall.

"Very good." The officer looked at the two policemen. "Why didn't we think earlier at it?"

"Or maybe better . . . a statue the holy Ho Chi Minh?"

"That's really brilliant, my loyal son! You make such a great progress in your re-education. You'll get a promotion very soon."

"Can it be, master, that I already feel the eternal joy of being a member of the communist family?"

"What you feel is real Communist happiness. That's the most wonderful feeling on earth. Many people are looking for it all of their life . . . without finding it. From now on nobody will ever take that feeling away from you."

Van Loi bowed and the curtain fell. All the actors got a standing ovation.

But downstairs several real agents were waiting for them. An officer took Van Loi by his collar. "You're under arrest."

"On . . . what charge?"

The man hit him in his face. "Propaganda against the regime."

Van Loi saw Van Ly in the corridor and cried, "Pray for me. They're going to destroy me."

The officer put his revolver in Van Loi's face, "Never laugh at Communism again or I'll kill you."

Van Loi acquiesced helplessly as officers pushed him into a police car. He was sentenced to seven years in prison.

"Where has the time gone? I can't believe it's been thirty years since they dragged you away," I said breathlessly. The squeaky wheels of my walker were echoing down the hallway.

"Visiting the chapel of the archdiocese at midnight made me happy," Van Loi said enthusiastically. "Because prayer unites us. Shouldn't you wait to light the second candle of the Advent wreath? It's only Thursday!"

"Of course, but I'm looking forward to Christmas."

"Yet I mainly feel anxiety."

"What's wrong?"

I looked downward. "Ever since the beginning of Advent a question has tormented me: What will my future be now that I have to go back to the concentration camp? And what will happen to Vietnam?"

Back in my room, I collapsed in my chair. It took me a few minutes to catch my breath.

We were sitting next to each other without saying a word.

"I draw a lot of strength from your presence."

"There's more than that," Van Loi mused. "Enormous strength lies in silence. But in hectic times, people are not interested in silence. Yet nothing is stronger than silence. And nothing is as powerful as the silence of the night."

Moments later, Van Loi yawned and got up. "This is . . . our farewell." He was unable to say anything else.

I put on my glasses, and I combed my hair with my stiff fingers. Drops of sweat glistened on his forehead, and his eyes were wet. For the first time in a long time, we hugged—he, the little priest in his black cassock, and I, slender and a head taller in my beige pajamas.

As I opened the door, we softly sang the *Song of Peace* by Kim Long:

> Lord, teach me to love and serve God.
> Make me an instrument of your peace.
> Where there is hatred, let me sow love . . .

In the corridor, Lieutenant Colonel Kien, my head guard, was startled as if he had been caught. He was apparently asleep. With automatic reflex this forty-year-old stout man with chubby cheeks adjusted his cap and tie and caressed his insignia: two stars and a bar.

Leaning against the doorframe I tried to give myself courage. "Our peaceful struggle . . . for freedom . . . continues," I said seemingly in a firm voice.

"Five years . . . another five years in Camp *Nam Ha*." The voice of the always so determined Van Loi vibrated suddenly. "I'm worried . . . about your health. Will we ever see each other again?"

I looked him straight in the eye, half whispering, "It is becoming an uphill battle, because four strokes have left me half paralyzed. But you're right. We will remain united in prayer." I continued, trembling. "Even when I will no longer be here," I turned my gaze skyward, "I will continue to support you, along with Nguyen Kim Dien, our murdered Archbishop."

"Be assured. We will continue to campaign," reassured Van Loi in a soothing voice. "Tomorrow, I'm going to the prayer vigil at the Redemptorist monastery in *Thai Ha* in Hanoi." And as the Lietenant Colonel looked on, he continued, "And we'll continue to sign the letters of our Priest Association in your name also."

I nodded. "Do those letters make sense anymore? Huu Giai and Chan Tin are old. Why don't any young priests defy this regime? Why should each prospective seminarian accept the blessing of the Communist Party? When will this government meddling stop?"

"You should think less, and we should act more," Van Loi replied confidently. He pulled a small packet out of his briefcase. "Here, for the road," he said with a lump in his throat.

In the corridor he didn't look back. This farewell was too difficult for him. The creaking of his sandals died out as he went down the stairs.

I shuffled to the window of my room behind my walker and saw him step into his old Renault. How many years has he had that car now? Amongst the impatiently honking motorbikes, he drove onto the bridge and over the canal. Behind it, the towers of Hue Cathedral stand like lighthouses.

On April 30, 1974, together with three colleagues, I was prostrate on the steps of the choir. My whole family dressed in their best clothes in the first row. For my parents, staunch Catholics, donating their youngest son to the church was a form of extreme obedience. For me, the priesthood meant the culmination of eleven years of training.

June, 27, 1963. My childhood friend Truc accompanied me to the entrance of the seminary, where the yellow and white papal flags hung from the facade.

"Do you see those cranes towering above the city? They're building the cathedral," Truc proudly said when he rang the doorbell. It echoed in the corridor. "Success! See you later."

"I have a meeting with President Nguyen Van Thuan."

The hunchbacked handyman who opened the door didn't utter a word as he led me to the President's office. His room impressed me. Bookshelves along the wall contained hundreds of neatly arranged books, but chaos reigned on his writing table. The smell of new books and pipe tobacco hung in the air.

"Never mind the mess," he said with a disarming smile. "As editor of seminary journal, I have to check all the citations and references."

"The letter of recommendation from my pastor," I said meekly. Already 16 years old, I was a so-called late vocation.

He read the letter carefully.

"Tell me, when did you first think of becoming a priest?" This colossus with black hair and thick glasses interrogated me. He sat at his desk with his back to the window and the desk lamp was pointed at my face.

"I have been thinking about it for a long time. I've always loved pretending that I'm a priest for boys and girls of the neighborhood. On a kitchen chair, there would be a glass of water beside which would lay a piece of bread and my mother's missal. An old bedspread served as a chasuble."

I rarely found myself searching for words, but I was babbling.

"I have no explanation, but in the past year, the dream of becoming a priest has come to the surface again."

"Tell me. Has something special happened?"

"Nothing in particular. My friend next door, Truc, is already in the seminary, and our pastor is very enthusiastic. I want to follow in his footsteps."

Van Thuan read the letter a second time put his chin between his thumb and index finger. "'A sharp intelligence, great tact, and a large dose of idealism.' Your pastor was my classmate. Sounds like he hasn't changed since I knew him. That makes me happy. When belief is authentically experienced, it generates enthusiasm."

Then the next question was fired at me.

"Tell me, what do you expect from the training?"

"I want to get to know Christ better, to be able to think and act like him. God says that you can only love him if you love your fellow human beings, and among them especially the outcasts. I grew up in poverty, but I've found that you can make the poor happy by being close to them. I'm ready to sacrifice my life for this."

Van Thuan nodded. "Do you know why the early believers were called Christians?"

He didn't give me time to answer the question.

"Because people recognized the Doctrine of Christ in their way of living. And yes, salt should have the taste of salt. You become a Christian only when Jesus's words also have an impact on your life. Authenticity, that's what it is about. What matters is who you really are—not who you claim to be. If people don't recognize the figure of Christ in you, you are not a Christian."

I remained speechless while the President filled his pipe and mulled over the letter. "The study of the Bible is so important because this unique book gives an answer to the questions of life. We must minimize the distance between the source that inspires us and our ways of living. Exactly like in the time of the Old Testament, we need prophets, people who teach us that we should not deviate from the truth, even though our country is torn by the civil war between North and South Vietnam."

"Please excuse me for saying so," I said, "but I grew up in a poor family, in an isolated village without a newspaper. I therefore have little understanding of politics."

"We'll teach you critical thinking. No problem," continued Van Thuan. "But you must always remember that there's only one way out. We must return to the roots of our faith. Look around you. How many deaths and injuries are there each day? I expect peace neither from the current leaders of North and South Vietnam nor from the South Vietnamese president Ngo Dinh Diem. I say that with regret in my heart because he's my uncle. Yet I believe that peace is possible. Peace begins within ourselves. When everyone is at peace with themselves, there will also be peace in our country and in the world."

"Now I understand why Truc speaks so enthusiastically about you." I reacted.

Van Thuan smiled. "Tell me, what was your parents' reaction?"

"Mama wept with happiness. For years she has been praying for a vocation in the family. Dad was not surprised. 'I just hope that your temper will not play tricks,' he said."

"We will soon know who we are dealing with."

I felt that he was seeing right through me. His handshake upon departure remained with me for a long time.

"Come back next month for the entrance exam."

With a warm feeling, I followed the hunchbacked man down the long hallway to the front door. I turned around one last time. Soon I would receive confirmation of the choice I had made in the depths of my heart.

"Hey, how was your meeting with Van Thuan?"

"He's got such a personality, and he's a real intellectual! I feel so insignificant and small."

"The training at the seminary is on a very high level," Truc assured me. "I'm sure about this. This is really your thing. You will like it over there."

On the street, I saw American advisers equipped with modern amenities for the first time. I stared.

"Is this the first time you've seen them?"

I nodded. "What does that soldier with his khaki beret have in his hand? A telephone?"

"Of course not. That's a walkie-talkie. Soldiers can talk to each other with them, even if they're on opposite sides of the city."

When we walked by, I only understood a few fragments of sentences because I only knew a few words of English.

"The Americans instill confidence in me, Truc."

"Why? Are you sure?" He looked surprised.

"Nobody has such state-of-the-art military equipment. And aren't they our brothers in Christ? I'm convinced that they will beat the hated Communists of the Viet Cong."

"Everyone hopes that they'll do that of course," Truc agreed. "But . . ."

"You eternal pessimist! Didn't you hear the words the U.S. President, John F. Kennedy, at the Berlin wall today? '*Ich bin ein Berliner.*' To me, Kennedy is not only a resident of Berlin but also of South Vietnam."

"After what has happened to my father, you know, my aversion to all forms of violence has grown even more. I don't like seeing more and more American advisors arriving over here."

"Yet not all things coming from the U.S.A. are bad." I argued. I took a can of corned beef out of my bag. "I don't have mustard, pickles, onions, or bread as the American soldiers have, but that cooked beef smells good. Taste!"

"Too salty," Truc said making a dismissive gesture.

"Come on. Don't exaggerate. There's nothing wrong with this meat."

I saw that he was deep in thought.

"I'm not talking about that meat," Truc challenged me. "The main question is whether more military force can lead to peace. And whether a Christian can justify the use of violence? I'm not blind. Very soon the Americans will participate in the war. I don't like them."

"But they really can stop the Viet Cong."

"I'm afraid that Vietnam will become the playground where the Americans and the communists will fight their Cold War. And the Vietnamese people will be the victim."

I did not know how to answer him.

"And that is just the tip of the iceberg," Truc continued. "For two weeks already, a revolt has paralyzed the country. Why did the police kill eight women and children during that peaceful demonstration by Buddhists? Their only request was to hang their flags for the celebration of the birth of Buddha. Why wasn't that allowed? Yet anywhere in the city, the papal flag can fly to celebrate the silver jubilee of our Archbishop. And after a monk had immolated himself in a street of Saigon, four others followed suit." He sighed. "What else will happen?"

While I was still pondering Truc's words, we saw a new demonstration by Buddhists from the steps of the cathedral.

"What's happening over there? Look at these monks in their orange robes proudly display their flags with a wheel drawn in the middle. Why are these so important to them?"

"The great wheel symbolizes the *Dharma*, or the teachings of Buddha. The spokes of the wheel evoke the eightfold path that each disciple traverses during his lifetime," Truc said. "Van Thuan will explain all that in his lessons."

Hundreds of heavily armed policemen in the middle of the bridge clearly signaled that the protesters were not allowed to enter the European quarter, and, although they did not intend to travel to this part of the city, the police charged. What a provocation! The sacred flags of the Buddhists were especially targeted. The cries of fear and panic were deafening. Before our eyes, we saw a bald monk and a woman holding up a protest sign being beaten.

Truc grabbed me by my shirt. "We must run now or we'll be beaten up too."

A few streets away Truc began to weep. "How do you justify such repression?"

What had been expected for months had finally happened. The South Vietnamese president Ngo Dinh Diem was assassinated in a coup, but his death was not a harbinger of a return to peace. Instead, South Vietnam became bogged down in a political stalemate, and the civil war became more terrible every day.

Almost all of my childhood memories are about this violence. After all, I lived near the demarcation line with the communist North Vietnam. Each trip to Hue was strewn with dangerous pitfalls. Sabotage, bombings, and firefights took place on the road leading to town almost every day.

Like on January 30, 1964, a day I will never forget.

I was sitting on the bus, on the way home, when an ambulance with a shrill siren sped past us, accompanied by two jeeps with South Vietnamese soldiers.

"Something terrible has happened." I told Truc. "Hopefully, it isn't too bad."

I held my breath when a little further along our bus was stopped by soldiers. On a stretch of the road, I saw pools of blood and spent bullet casings. A doctor and two nurses were trying to resuscitate the victims, but they had arrived on the scene too late. Truc held his hands over his eyes.

"I have to fulfill my duty as a Christian," I said.

"Don't do that," intervened Truc. "That's too dangerous."

Despite the ban, I managed to sneak up to the door of the bus.

"Stop or I'll shoot!" The soldier pointed his rifle barrel at me, but his hands were shaking.

I looked him straight in the eyes and felt that he was more scared than me. "I am a seminarian." My voice became louder. "These are not animals, but people. I'm going to say a prayer for them and sign their forehead with the sign of the cross. That is my moral duty."

With great difficulty I finally got close to the victims. On the side of the road, the bodies were covered with sheets that immediately became red with blood. I kneeled in front of a girl who was about eight years old. She was still holding on to her doll. Her face was partially blown off.

Anger swelled up inside of me. I raised my hands to the sky and began to cry. This was the first time since my childhood that I had been physically confronted with death. The only question that haunted my mind was "Why?" I broke into a cold sweat when I realized that this attack had taken place just ten minutes earlier. The unit of Viet Cong had, obviously, already disappeared.

The next day I read a short article in the newspaper. The District Officer and his wife were assassinated. They were the targets of that attack. But three bystanders were also killed. The Provincial Governor praised the fallen officer, "This was a conscientious man with a great sense of responsibility." A picture of another government official who was murdered in Saigon the day before also appeared on the same page.

I was shocked.

"Can you imagine, Truc?"

"I'm afraid so," he answers stoically. "The South Vietnamese army, as well as the Viet Cong, conduct raids daily. The difference is that you are now physically faced with it."

"The tone of the article is unbearable. It's as if these bystanders had just been unlucky, at the wrong people at the wrong place. Don't they have parents? And what would the future hold for their children now?"

"Of course you're right. But unfortunately there's a world of difference between being right and the triumph the righteousness. I hope and pray everyday that Vietnam will one day live in peace."

"I also do. But how can I put the image of the little girl with her doll out of my mind?"

Meanwhile, the coup by General Nguyen Khanh got all the attention in the media.

"I have only one purpose," said the man with the goatee beard and the uniform with three stars. "I want to give Vietnam a better future." He read this empty phrase off of a piece of paper that he got from his principals. I felt that he was even more corrupt than his predecessors whom he had executed.

"I will never use a weapon, Truc." I promise.

"It's easy for us to say, of course, because as seminarians we are exempt from military service."

"I made a final decision. I want to commit myself as a priest, body and soul, to fight for peace with nonviolent methods."

"Glad to hear that I'm not the only one."

Even before I celebrated my seventeenth birthday, my life's goals were firmly set.

With a thud, the little bundle of Van Loi fell from my hand. As always, at the slightest noise, Lieutenant Colonel Kien burst into my room.

"Thanks!" I laughed. "Did you think that I suffered a stroke again?"

Kien grimaced sourly.

"Oh, sorry. I almost forgot. I'm under house arrest."

The man yawned. His guard duty was almost over. As he had been taught, he kept his right hand on his shiny revolver. It hung prominently on his belt next to the golden buckle. The Communists know how to intimidate people. They constantly reminded me that I'd better not flee.

"Shouldn't you say goodbye?" I said, not without a touch of malice. "Life in the remote camp of Nam Ha will be quite different from what you're used to over here! What do you think? Where would you prefer to stay? Over here in this beautiful city or in the middle of the jungle?"

Kien turned around and left the room. He's too proud to show any emotion and too loyal to the system to which he owed everything.

In the seminary, especially at night, we heard the impact of bombs in the distance.

"You can't sleep?" I whisper.

Truc is tossing and turning in the bed next to mine.

"What do you want? The demarcation line is just forty miles away as the crow flies," I said.

"What does the U.S. President Johnson want to achieve with that incessant bombing?"

"To get the Communists on their knees; what else?"

"How many deaths will there be tonight? Why all that pointless violence?"

"You can't stop the war, Truc." This time we were awakened at five o'clock in the morning. "We can only try to become better human beings and demonstrate this to others as a priest. That's what we are doing every day through Holy Mass, meditation, lessons, and study. This is your only alternative."

"Do you believe that?"

"I'm absolutely certain of it."

"Self-control is a key word in your formation," Rector Van Thuan emphasized during class. "It's important to learn to control yourself and not immediately yield to whims. Voluntary celibacy is part of the priesthood; a priesthood in which you must pursue asceticism, also in food and drink."

"The latter is not hard," I whispered in Truc's ear.

He was biting on his tongue not to laugh.

"Think on celibacy with trust," continued Van Thuan, "and count on the state of grace. The key to all this is humor. Humor ensures that problems remain in perspective and reduces them to their correct proportions."

Sitting next to me, Truc sank deeply into thought.

"Sooner or later, every human being falls in love," said Van Thuan. "Yes, that could also happen to a seminarian or a priest. It hits you before you notice it. However, succumbing to this temptation is venturing on a slippery slope. It is best not to show that love, because as soon as the feeling is mutual, you attract unexpected trouble. You lose your serenity, balance, and inner peace. And you become unhappy. But be aware that these feelings wear off; love is like water-based paint, it disappears after a while."

One evening I had an appointment with Van Thuan.

"I'm trying to meet each seminarian every month, but I have so little time. How are you?"

"I'm fine."

"Tell me, how do you look back to your first six months at the seminary?"

"What I find most fascinating is the way we learn to think and pray through the study of philosophy and theology, the services, the literature, and personal interviews. I'm making my first steps in developing my spirituality and personal prayer. That is not so easy. But since we are learning to preach, I want to do this every day. Furthermore, the introduction to catechesis and Gregorian chant is an enrichment."

"It seems that you've found your feet over here. Persist in this way. And don't hesitate to contact me when you have questions."

But life is simply a series of ups and downs. And things were not always easy. The most difficult time was when fellow students gave up. They realized after an internal struggle that the priesthood was not really for them and left. It stunned me every time, because during our stay in the seminary a personal relationship would develop.

"I'm leaving tonight." Truc bowed his head and wept softly.

We grew up as neighbors, and I joined him here when he had already been in the seminary for four years. But now we went out separate ways. I could hardly believe it. I hugged him for several minutes. "I felt in recent months that your thoughts were often elsewhere. You think I have never doubted my vocation?"

"After the early death of my dad, I feel an enormous need for affection and tenderness," said Truc. "No, I don't think I can handle celibacy. I can't live in solitude. With you it's different. You're so much stronger mentally. You draw strength from the silence, while I lose myself in it."

The bell rang; study started. Upset, I was the last person to enter the study room. Truc saw that and before leaving, he sneaked into the study and put his passport photo on my table. On the back of the photo he had written, "My heart will always be with you."

That same evening I went to the office of Rector Van Thuan, my spiritual father.

"It's normal that you are confused at such a critical moment. All I can do is prescribe some spiritual medicine. You can draw much strength from regularly going to Confession, and you will learn how to meditate."

"In view of my temperament, I don't think this will be self-evident."

"What you need is an iron discipline. And you have that. You must create silence in your heart—push everything aside—and contemplate your inner evolution. By this, you learn to speak with the "Other," the great mystery Jesus calls Father. Try to feel God's presence. In order to give content to your meditation, prepare it before bedtime. Try it. You will see. This approach works. I wish you good luck!"

To this day, I still continue to note down a thought before bedtime.

Near the seminary, in the heart of the European district of Hue, the broad boulevards and colonial buildings still breathed the grandeur of French imperialism.

Every Sunday afternoon, I walked with Truc to the Imperial Citadel on the other side of the river. Emperor Gia Long built this gigantic complex after the unification of Vietnam in 1802. I was impressed by the size, the pageantry, and the splendor. The beating heart, the "forbidden" Purple City, was originally exclusively reserved for the emperor and his entourage, but the area was in decline when I went there for the first time. In this haven of tranquility, birds and butterflies reigned.

"I can't understand why Gia Long was inspired by the Forbidden City in Beijing," I said. "Isn't China our hereditary enemy? For the past two thousand years, the shadow of the Chinese Empire has hung over Vietnam, and we've been a colony for centuries."

"You're right about that," Truc said. "Each time the Vietnamese people wrestled independence from China, the kings paid an annual tribute to the Chinese emperor. That feeling of superiority . . . I do not like the Chinese either."

The door of my room swung open. The doorknob slammed against the wall.

My frightened bodyguard, Phuc, who took over from the Lieutenant Colonel, didn't see me in the bed; I was standing in front of the window. "Damn it, you're not sleeping yet?"

"Did you think that I had run away?" I said grinning. "That would be bad for your career!"

The man shook his head. "Go to bed. Tomorrow I'll call you up. At five."

"I know that you monitor me day and night, but that the regime now also determines when I should go to bed is news to me. It would not surprise me to learn that the newly appointed parliament of puppets is debating this issue. All communists are obsessed with the idea that citizens should be more restricted."

My aversion to this uncouth man with a greasy pompadour and the rank of sergeant is strong. He thinks that he can look forward to a great career by faithfully serving his paymasters. "How old are you, that you think you can lecture me?"

He adjusted the tie of his green uniform. "Born in 1968 when the *Tet* offensive marked the end of American imperialism," he beamed with a greasy smile.

I turned my head. His breath stank. He hadn't brushed his teeth.

"What do you know about *Tet*, except for the fables in the falsified history books?"

Being unable to formulate a response, Phuc was pissed off and returned to his chair in the corridor.

"Why is *Tet* is the greatest feast of the year, Mom?"

"That's the evidence itself, my little boy. It's the beginning of the new lunar year and springtime, and also the feast of ancestor worship. Every Vietnamese celebrates *Tet*."

"Even the communists in the North?"

"I . . . actually don't know. We know nothing about them. You should ask Dad when he comes in from the fields. But, I think so. . . . Hmm, yes, I'm sure they do."

"Why do we offer for our ancestors incense sticks, fruit, and flowers?"

"What do you think? To appease their spirits, of course. You know that! Because they still affect our everyday life. I'm going to clean the family grave. Will you give me a helping hand?"

After our return, I went to play again with some improvised toys.

"Hey, our job isn't finished yet. Now we have to decorate the house and the family altar. And we must clean the shelves with the pictures of our deceased grandparents. You see, they are smiling on us."

"Does every ancestor have their own self?"

"Of course!"

"Tell me a story of each of them!"

Mom sighed. "A very short one, because there's also the family dinner tonight."

In the evening the whole family was there, including my oldest brother Nguyen San with his wife and children. He was twenty-one years older than me. Uncles, aunts, nephews, and nieces joined us also at the festive table. The family home was bursting at the seams. We didn't often come together, but it was always a cordial reunion. For a while, the war was forgotten and joys and sorrows are shared. To my grandfather and grandmother, *Tet* was the most beautiful day of the year.

Everyone brought food, and, after drinking several glasses of *bia hoi*, the atmosphere was boisterous. When my oldest brother began to sing, we shrieked with laughter. It was a popular song from his childhood about a duck:

> One duck opens its two wings,
> It says quack, quack, quack, quack, quack, quack,
> It jumps into a pond . . .

Everyone made the corresponding gestures and sang along cheerfully. Even my father, who was always fully absorbed in social discussions, joined in.

"Mom and Dad, I wish you a prosperous and happy life," I said.

Finally, I got my long awaited gift and opened it in an instant.

"Wow! A real car!" I exclaimed.

"Well, not a real car, it's made of wood." Dad laughed.

But I was as proud as a peacock. This became my dearest possession.

I was allowed to stay up until after midnight. Before the family altar, we always gave thanks to our ancestors. At midnight, we finished the feast with both a round and a square rice cake.

"Where is the *ruou de*?" asked my oldest brother, Nguyen San. "No *Tet* without a toast with rice alcohol."

Every year Mom would warn us to "be careful with the porcelain cups. These family heirlooms and are only used once a year. They must serve for eternity."

Afterwards, the village feast started. I watched the fireworks with awe.

"The evil spirits flee at the sound of firecrackers," Mom said while putting me to bed. As I fell asleep, I clutched my wooden car.

Traditionally, *Tet* was regarded as a short-term respite during the civil war. And every year the seminary took a two-week break.

"Will you come celebrate *Tet* in Saigon?" Nguyen Tri, the older brother, who was working in Saigon, invited me in 1968.

"I can't refuse. I've never been to the capital."

After the banquet, at midnight, my brother opened the windows of his apartment. "Your eyes will fall wide open," he laughed. "Fireworks in Saigon are quite different from the fireworks in Ba Ngoat."

Awestruck, I watched the glittering spectacle that illuminated the sky.

"But don't I hear bombs falling?" I asked aghast.

I had just spoken when dull thuds could be heard nearby.

"That's near the presidential palace around the corner," my brother said, bewildered.

"Shall we go and have a look?" I asked. "Maybe we can help people?"

"Are you mad?"

More detonations followed.

"This must be an attack by the Viet Cong."

Soon the sound of gunfire from elsewhere in the city stopped the revelry.

"What's happening here?" my brother said. "Wasn't there a cease-fire?"

Nguyen Tri was still confused. "Father is right. You can never trust the communists." And he ordered, "Switch on the radio!"

We picked up a North Vietnamese station. "All over the country a spontaneous popular uprising against the corrupt puppet regime of the Americans has erupted." Everyone was frightened. "We call on all residents of the South to support the uprising. You are about to be saved!" After this message, communist battle-songs were broadcast.

On TV we learned that in a surprise attack, the Viet Cong had attacked military barracks, police stations, and government buildings in more than a hundred places. "The building that housed the TV station was also targeted, but that attack was repelled. And a counter-offensive is being launched. Stay inside." The TV presenter said.

The next day I heard a testimony from Hue. "Thousands of civil servants, politicians, religious leaders, and even foreigners were executed, burned alive, or bound hand and foot and dumped in mass graves," said an upset man.

The spontaneous popular uprising did not happen, but quite the contrary. A massive reaction came from the Americans and South Vietnamese troops. I saw trucks carrying loads of slain Viet Cong fighters to mass graves. I still shiver when I recall that image. Any sense of humanity had disappeared.

In the evening the media widely reported these "successes."

"What's happening over here, brother? First the North Vietnamese propaganda and now South Vietnamese propaganda. The media coverage about the war is one big lie and sheer manipulation. The 'good cause' they fight for is nothing more than ideological propaganda."

"You're only understanding that now?" he said to my surprise. "Propaganda is an essential part of not only our society but of all societies. It has always been like that in history. And you can't change that; believe me. Despite everything, we can consider ourselves lucky that we are living in South Vietnam and not in the North."

"You were right," I told Truc later.

"That's the first time you've said that," he joked.

"You were already skeptical of the Americans in 1963. Despite their superior weaponry and the incessant bombing, they are not our saviors. The *Tet* Offensive hit them in the heart. This is a turning point. It will be impossible for the Americans to win the war. Although they were decimated, the communist Viet Cong are the moral victors."

"Do you still like corned beef?" laughed Truc while he ran away.

I threw my shoe at his head.

I'm lying on my bed, but cannot sleep.

In the closet with the door slightly ajar, I see the glow of the streetlights on my black cassock. I will definitely pack my cassock in my suitcase tomorrow.

Moments later, I get up. I carefully fold my cassock and rub the buttons. I don't have to count them. There are 33 buttons, as are the number of years in Jesus's life.

No, I do not regret that I followed in his footsteps. If I had to start all over again, I'd do the same, even though I know that anyone who consistently defends the truth is still being mercilessly persecuted. During the past two thousand years, little has actually changed. The Communists do not kill us, but let us rot slowly, as if we were the lepers of modern times. But whatever may happen, I'll continue to stand up for the truth.

My cassock still felt new when, in 1968, I entered the major seminary. I only had a short time to unpack all my stuff, because we were immediately expected in the chapel for a ceremony. Being sprayed by the aspergillum followed a prayer formula in Latin. After Ordination, I could finally wear my cassock.

Back from the chapel, the "transformation" took place. Civilian clothes were stored in the closet, and I put on a cassock. Closing all the buttons was a complicated chore, and putting on the Roman collar was not easy either; it takes getting used to.

In full regalia, we were ready for our first public appearance. Doesn't someone say: fine feathers make fine birds? I was the first to enter the recreation area. The older students companions judged me, their words laced with witticisms.

Someone pulled on the rope around my waist while another observed: "Is there water in your basement?" He pulled down my cassock.

When my colleagues trickled in, they were also noisily and critically judged.

Nevertheless, the black robe was an outward sign of our dignity. We now belonged to a privileged caste. On the street, some bowed or removed their hats while others made a detour so as not to cross me or look upon me as a marginalized person.

According to the beliefs of the time, people dressed in a cassock were above the common man and knew everything better. Back then, the priest officiated in the church with his back turned to the people and still climbed the pulpit.

But I especially wanted to mingle with people and lead by example in the fight against poverty and for peace and justice. This difference of opinion led in 1969 to heated discussions with the person responsible for our spiritual training. This "holy priest" had a penchant for sentimental devotion.

"You always think you know everything better," said the professor as our umpteenth debate reached boiling point. His textbook plopped down on the desk.

"Revolutionary! Your place is in the army and not in the seminary. Where are we going if devotion to Mary and the saints no longer occupy a central place in the life of priests!"

"The saints and especially Our Lady of La Vang are dear to me, but this devotion only fuels my commitment. Our mission is rooted in the real world, right?"

The bell signaled the end of the class. I was the last person to leave the classroom.

"Professor," I said, "for months now I have followed your lessons with a bitter feeling. I want to discuss the matter with our Rector."

"After Compline," he said cautiously, "Tell me what bothers you."

Nguyen Van Thuan listened to the arguments of both parties. After some thought, he said, "The image of God, every believer tries to grasp it. Some do that through contemplation, others by action. At first sight, your ideas are diametrically opposed, but that is not so. You are both climbing the same mountain, but from different sides. Both of you hope to reach the top. But the top remains inaccessible because God is infinitely greater than we are."

I was impressed by so much wisdom and insight.

"Asking which one of the two paths is the best is a false question," he continued. "The most important thing is to allow the Spirit of God to penetrate deep within yourself." Van Thuan began to look for something on his permanently chaotic desk. "That booklet. Where did I put it? I recently read the writings of the thirteenth-century Persian writer Muhammad Rumi." Van Thuan took off his glasses. "I believe the mystics become the closest to God in all religious traditions." Moments later, he found what he wanted and began to read, "I have travelled the world seeking God and I have not found him anywhere. When I came back home, I saw him at the door of my heart. And he said, 'Here I have been waiting for you for eons.' Then I entered the house with Him."

Van Thuan closed the booklet. "One way. There is only one way to happiness. That is to find God within yourself. That's the issue."

I got up and bowed.

"One moment," the Rector ordered. "Before you leave, I want you to listen to a piece of music that sums up everything and will give you food for thought."

He set up his old phonograph and took a vinyl record with Ludwig van Beethoven's *Ninth Symphony*, performed by Herbert von Karajan.

"At the time he completed his last symphony, Beethoven was completely deaf, but it became his crowning achievement. This work reflects his suffering and despair, but especially his dream that one day all men will become brothers. Listen to the finale!"

> Your magic brings together
> What custom has sternly divided.
> All men shall become brothers,
> Wherever your gentle wings hover.

Without a word, we returned to our rooms.

I went back to bed and turned painfully onto one side. Because of my paralysis, it was difficult to find the right position for sleeping. The twilight lit up a photo on the wall of my inspiring example, Redemptorist Brother Van.

He stayed in the monastery of Thai Ha in Hanoi after the division between North and South Vietnam in 1955. Today, that same monastery is once again the center of the resistance against the communist regime. Everyday for several weeks there, thousands of believers demonstrate peacefully against the plans for the construction of a wastewater treatment plant next to the church. This plant is intended to serve Dong Da Hospital that the government has set up in the former monastery. Last month the presence of thousands of Catholics who were mobilized by the chimes of the church bells prevented the storming of the site by the police. Since then a tense atmosphere hangs around Thai Ha.

Brother Van. His consistent peaceful thinking and acting fascinate me. But more than half a century ago the Communists sentenced him to fifteen years hard labor. After suffering torture and brainwashing, and having been locked in solitary confinement in a re-education camp, he died due to tuberculosis. The word "compromise" was not in his dictionary. This is how I want to live and how I always will, whatever may happen. I have learned that I will pay with my life for this attitude.

2

5:00 a.m.

"It's time!"

Still half asleep I pretended that I didn't hear Phuc.

"Damn it. We leave in one hour."

When he grabbed me by my pajamas, I didn't react immediately. I pushed him away. "You've no right to touch me."

Getting up was difficult. The melody of the *Song of Peace* by Kim Long still lingered in my head: "Make me an instrument of your peace." I thought of Van Loi who was now going to Thai Ha in Hanoi to attend a prayer vigil this evening.

I was still sitting on the edge of the bed when the Secretary of the Archbishop knocked on the half-open door. My Advent wreath wobbled when the door swung open. The light of the lamp illuminated the purple ribbon, a symbol of penance and repentance. I realized that my penance was to begin today. But will the Communists ever repent?

"Dearest colleague. I bring you greetings from our Archbishop, who wishes you a safe journey," said the man who hesitated as he put his hands around mine.

At first, I didn't know how to react, but I smiled.

"Why can't the Archbishop come and greet me and wish me a safe trip himself?"

"His Lordship wanted to greet you personally yesterday." The secretary tried to calm me down. "But his visitors stayed longer than expected."

"Any explanation seems acceptable. The Archbishop knows I never go to bed before midnight. Does he not understand the importance of this moment? This is my farewell to Hue. My rickety body will not survive another five years of imprisonment. What new compromise did he sign with the Communists?" was my biting comment.

"Now you are imagining things. His uncle and aunt from Da Nang were visiting him. You know very well that His Lordship is an advocate of a gentle approach because this produces better results than your hard line. Religious freedom has increased in recent years."

"Don't make me laugh. What does this freedom mean? Even before the sun has risen, I will return to the concentration camp."

"Pessimism does not help us move forward. After 35 years, we are once again active in schools, hospitals, orphanages, and institutions for the disabled. And we also take care of HIV patients. The six seminaries count 1,500 candidates for the priesthood, and restrictions on the pilgrimage to La Vang, which is so dear to you, have been lifted."

"A zero result makes you happy. Lenin believed that the idea of the existence of God is an unspeakable horror and an awful plague. And the current rulers are still as merciless as their mentor. Don't try to reach a compromise with a regime that, for decades, has destroyed every form of religion and now makes some opportunistic concessions."

I pointed trembling to the cathedral. "How many Catholics, who had desperately taken refuge there during the *Tet* Offensive, were killed?

The secretary didn't answer right away.

"Were that four hundred or five hundred people?"

"Dearest colleague, let us not quarrel when we say goodbye," sighed the secretary, while he helped me button up my shirt.

"Don't bother too much, because tonight I'll have to wear prison clothes."

"Remember the good times. You had a good time here anyway, right? After your stroke, we've taken good care of you."

His smooth talking got on my nerves.

"In the refrigerator in the kitchen you will find a portion of *banh khoai*," he whispered. "You'll like that pancake. Next to it is a jar of your favorite peanut sesame sauce."

"Thanks for that last supper."

"Look at things positively, dear colleague." He tried to reassure me "Do you know that . . ."

"You can talk, you. How many years have you spent in the camps? Since the Communist takeover in 1975, I've spent eighteen, with an additional fourteen years of house arrest with greased pompadours who watch you day and night."

Phuc, with his pointed chin in the door opening, listened intently to our conversation. In anger I burst out, "Can you count how long I've lived in freedom? Do you know how to count?"

During the final offensive of 1975 the retreat of the South Vietnamese troops without the backing of the Air Force was a debacle. Hundreds of thousands of soldiers were killed or captured during desperate fighting. On March 30, the port city of Da Nang, where two million refugees had gathered, fell.

The road to Saigon was now wide open. While some units with the courage of despair offered resistance, the country fell into the grip of a psychosis of fear. It was buzzing with rumors of massacres in the conquered territories. Day by day these stories became more gruesome. But who could distinguish truth from fiction? An unstoppable flow of refugees moved from the North to Saigon.

"Will you pick up my wife and children at my house?" Nguyen Tri anxiously asked over the telephone. "Go to the headquarters of the State Security. Use the back door to get in. The situation is dramatic here."

There was a lot of activity around the building. On the roof, American helicopters flew to and fro. Only with great difficulty we got inside. We walked through the corridors and up the stairs. In the courtyard heaps of documents were being burned. They were even thrown out of the windows.

"You're going to leave soon," my brother told his wife and children to reassure them. "There is a naval vessel off the coast. That ship is leaving for the United States."

"Are you leaving too?" I asked.

"I don't know . . . I'm the head of department over here . . . But do I have a choice in the matter? If the Communists would discover that I've worked here, they'll surely kill me."

"How great is the risk?"

"Very big," he said dejectedly. "Our service is infiltrated by agents of the Viet Cong. Like the doormen downstairs. They record everything that happens."

"But you can also join us, brother," he assured me.

I shook my head. "No, I'm waiting for orders from my bishop. He's my boss. He decides."

"At home I also have a boss," Nguyen Tri smiled. "But it is I that take this decision now." His wife blushed a deep red, but he immediately added, "It was only a joke."

"This is not the time to make jokes," she said with tears in her eyes as she firmly hugged her children.

"Sorry, you are right." Nguyen Tri heaved a deep sigh. "Yesterday I wanted to visit father and mother in Quang Bien, but I could not possibly leave here."

"But don't worry," I reassured him. "I just came from there. Many people have fled the village. But all is quiet over there. Father and mother are doing well. Our big brother San and our sister Hieu will take care of them. "

The door swung open. "Next flight in about two minutes! Leave now!" commanded a senior officer.

"I want to . . ." my brother said haltingly.

"No goodbyes," commanded the man.

"Hold on to your car," I patted my cousin's head. "Once I also got a gift from your father. This is your most treasured possession!" Sheepishly he looked back while the others had already rounded the corner.

"I only have ten employees left," said Archbishop Nguyen Kim Dien in a panicky voice on the telephone. "And only seven of my hundred and twenty priests remain at their posts. All the others have fled. Is your presence as Chaplain of the Society of Missionaries in Saigon still necessary? Over here in Hue, you would be of great help."

"No one is irreplaceable," I answered him.

In Saigon, I used my remaining money to buy a plane ticket to Da Nang. Dressed in my cassock, I took the last flight to the North with a few other passengers.

The customs officers didn't trust me. They stuck their nose in a small bottle of holy oil and, rummaging through my bag, they only found some clothes, a prayer book, and a copy of the New Testament.

On arrival, troop movements severely disrupted my onward journey. It took me seven days to travel the last hundred kilometers. I travelled by car, by pushcart, and in a railway carriage that was pulled by a horse. I found a rusty bicycle but it broke after a few kilometers. Along the way I took care of the wounded and administered the Last Rites to the dying. Some scenes seemed to come straight out of the Apocalypse, the description of the end of the world by John the Evangelist.

As I did not even have a single piastre, I managed to pay for room and board by working one night in the kitchen of a restaurant. The next day, I exchanged my New Testament for a bowl of *pho* soup in a bar.

"It'll help you overcome the bad times," I told the woman.

She smiled. This was the first smile I had seen in weeks.

I continued my journey on foot, and I was swimming in the South China Sea when an army patrol turned up. Luckily I stayed out of their sight.

A fisherman took me to the port of Thuy Duong. The first North Vietnamese soldiers I met were courteous. They allowed me to continue my journey to Hue.

On March 25, I arrived in the Archdiocese. The hunchback man who opened the door made wide gestures. He thought I was crazy, but the Archbishop cordially welcomed me.

"You're a man of my heart"

The next day, long columns of North Vietnamese troops marched through the European neighborhood. At the same place where twelve years earlier I had seen American advisers brimming with confidence, I now saw silent and shabbily dressed soldiers marching through the town. Their stay in the jungle visibly had affected their health.

In the South, hundreds of thousands of people, led by President Nguyen Van Thieu, left the country. However, many people didn't succeed in leaving the country. On April 30, Communist troops marched through the deserted streets of Saigon.

"Are you ready?" asked Kien in his plush, ironed uniform and Sunday shirt. The man exuded a sense of responsibility. In a conversation of his superior that I accidentally heard years ago, I could deduce that Kien had studied at the Institute of Marxist-Leninist Studies in Hanoi. That's the breeding ground of party leaders. But he has had to take a step back. What happened? Kien never said a word about it.

Clinging to my walker, I put my cassock, as well as some clothes, toilet utensils, my missal, photographs, and Van Loi's gift into my travel bag. In the small pile of letters, my eyes were drawn to the picture of my First Holy Communion, a few letters from Mom when I was in the seminary and in the camps, and a photo of my father and myself. "The two rock-hard heads," I read on the back. I recognized the handwriting of my sister Thi Hieu.

I opened a letter of congratulations that I had received from Hieu on the occasion of my priestly ordination. "Jesus compared the Kingdom of God to a mustard seed. This smallest seed on earth grows into a large mustard tree that yields thousands of fruits if planted in good soil and given much water and light. This is what I wish you during your priesthood. And whatever will happen, I will always be on your side. Warm greetings. Your loving sister."

I clenched my teeth. "Van Loi is right," I muttered. "No matter how difficult the situation of the Catholics in Vietnam, we shouldn't give up the fight. No, me too I shouldn't throw in the towel. Not for the Secretary of the Archbishop. For nobody!"

The last document I put in my travel bag was an envelope with the Coat of Arms of the Archdiocese. It was my appointment as Secretary of Archbishop Nguyen Kim Dien. I closed my eyes.

"Bring a message of reconciliation and cooperation," the Archbishop recommended when he asked me to write a draft for an open letter to the new rulers.

"Already an expression of sympathy for the Communists?"

"No, I've seen too many horrors. But you noticed in the eyes of the North Vietnamese soldiers who marched in the streets here that they are downright tired of this war. Finally peace and tranquility can return. We must insist on religious freedom which is guaranteed by the Constitution of North Vietnam."

"Don't delude yourself. I don't trust the Communists at all."

"Give them the benefit of the doubt."

"A search warrant!" Secret Service Agents pushed aside the hunchbacked gatekeeper and noisily burst into the Archbishop's palace. "You stand guard at the front door," the leader ordered three armed men, "and don't let anyone in. All others follow me."

"May I ask what's happening here?" I said.

The leader consulted his paper. "Are you Bishop Nguyen Kim Dien?"

"His secretary."

"Where is Dien?"

"Monsignor is in his office on the first floor. And who may I announce," I said while I tried to stop the men from mounting the stairs.

"That's none of your business," the leader snapped.

Two agents stood guard in front of the office of the Archbishop. The leader and two other men interrogated him.

I regularly peeked out into the hallway, but the situation remained unchanged for hours. Around noon, I took a folder under my arm, and I went to the office.

"His Lordship has to sign these letters," I said to one of the agents.

He knocked on the door and an interrogator came out. Through the half-open door, I saw the dazed Archbishop.

"The outgoing mail," I stammered.

"The Archbishop currently has other things on his mind."

"Should I come back later?"

"Everything depends on his cooperation. We're not on the same wavelength yet, but we'll get there," said the man laughing. "I'll let you know when we're ready."

It was half past seven in the evening when the interrogators finally left.

The Archbishop looked like a beaten dog. "This is absurd! I had to answer the same questions in writing over and over again. The versions were compared, and a discussion then ensued about the differences."

"Well, that was that. We're rid of them."

"That's what you think! They'll be back tomorrow."

"To do what?"

"That's what I'm asking myself too."

"Try to put all that out of your head. Don't you want to watch the news program on TV?"

"Yes, the English language Channel 11."

"Impossible. It doesn't exist anymore!"

"And Channel 9?"

"What's happening here? These are new presenters. And they speak with a North Vietnamese accent."

The next day at eight o'clock Secret Service agents burst into the Archbishop's office again.

"And this time you won't disturb us," the leader snarled.

But I didn't let him put me off. "Can I be of any help monsignor?"

"Deliver this letter to the principal of the Quoc Hoc-College and go to our institutions in the poorest areas of the city. Prepare a report on their greatest needs."

The smell of burnt books hung in the air of the streets of Hue. A truck delivered a new load from the university library. Under the all-seeing eyes of soldiers, students enthusiastically threw the books on a large bonfire. "Fortunately, yesterday, we moved all the important books of our library to a safe place," I thought.

I saw that members of the Youth League cut the long hair of passersby. There was no getting away from it. And in the streets, workers placed loudspeakers at every twentieth house. Soon the loudspeakers incessantly broadcast songs praising Ho Chi Minh, socialism, and revolution.

I asked for *Tin Sang* at the newsstand.

"Don't you know that all South Vietnamese newspapers were banned yesterday? I only have *Nhan Dan*, the mouth piece of the communist party, and the newspaper of the Youth League."

"No, thank you," I said astonished. There were also stacks of books for sale with the writings of Ho Chi Minh, Marx, Engels and Lenin, and books about the achievements of the Communist Party.

"Have you sold much today?"

The man didn't reply.

An immense portrait of Ho Chi Minh was hung on the facade of the Quoc Hoc-College.

"Why the portrait?" I asked the receptionist.

"Don't you know that our historic leader attended school over here?"

"Eh, no. Are you new here?"

She laughed. "Everyone is new here. And you are?"

"The Secretary of the Archbishop."

"A bishop, you said. What is that?"

"I've come to deliver a personal letter to the principal," I mumbled.

"He's coming down the stairs." I saw a man who was neatly dressed in a custom-made suit.

I was completely bewildered. "Since when have you been the principal?"

"Since yesterday."

"Where is Mr. Truong, your predecessor?"

"He is attending a 'ten-day class.' As soon as their minds are purified from the cultural and ideological contamination of which they have been victims, they can get back to work," the man smiled.

He addressed his secretary. "Please send the driver of the removal van from Hanoi to the principal's residence next door. My wife is waiting for him."

In the classes I passed by when leaving the building, children were singing militant communist songs. Is this their new morning prayer?

Back in my room, I listened secretly to *The Voice of America*. Thich Quang Do, the leader of the underground association of Buddhists, said, "We will never become slaves of the Communist Party." He was arrested the same day. In protest against the religious persecution, twelve Buddhist monks and nuns set themselves on fire. But I did not see any pictures of it on TV.

The clever form of state control that quietly usurped our society perplexed me. Communist administrators were appointed in our orphanages, nursing homes, and institutions for the disabled. The seminaries became training centers for communists and all religious properties were nationalized. To make way for the invasion of North Vietnamese and to relieve pressure on the cities, millions of South Vietnamese were ordered to move to the New Economic

Zones. For the deported Catholics abandoned to their fate, together with some colleagues, I wrote the manual, *I Live Happily*.

A week before the fall of South Vietnam, Pope Paul VI had appointed Nguyen Van Thuan, my former rector at the seminary, to be Archbishop of Saigon. But he also ended up behind bars. Later, I helped to put the messages he had written in prison in the book *The Road of Hope*.

The interrogations of the Archbishop continued for 120 days. Everyday I assisted him as much as possible.

"Keep your spirits up!" I said. "Prayer is the most powerful weapon against such psychological terror."

"Do you think I'm doing something else," he answered irritatedly. "The Communists do not want reconciliation, only install a terrible tyranny."

"Prime Minister Pham Van Dong is willing to receive you, my lord." I gave him the letter.

"That surprises me. I never thought he was going to answer my letter. But I want you to come with me."

The rainy season had just ended when we took the train to Hanoi on a sunny November morning.

"Our security is guaranteed," I said in a whisper. I had recognized four agents of the Secret Service in our wagon. We communicated in writing, exchanging small pieces of paper.

At the station, the secretary of the Archbishop of Hanoi awaited us.

"Finally we can talk freely," sighed Dien in the office of his colleague. But the man pointed his finger to the ceiling and the wall. Here every conversation was overheard.

"Shall we prepare ourselves for the six o'clock Mass?" The Archbishop of Hanoi winked.

"It's only half past five," I remarked.

"It is necessary to prepare well for the service," Monsignor Dien said, giving me a poke in the back. The vestry was the only place where they could talk freely.

I stood guard in the choir, and I knocked on the door when two acolytes of course Secret Agents arrived.

When Mass started, I noticed my boss had lost his composure.

After dinner, we walked in the garden. "After the Communist takeover in 1955, terrible things have happened here," he whispered, distressed. "The church has been decimated, and I fear that we do not fully understand what is awaiting us. The Communists have only one goal: to exterminate all religions."

The office of Prime Minister Pham Van Dong in a former French residence was crammed with books. We noticed the works of all the great French writers: Victor Hugo, Emile Zola, Jean-Paul Sartre, and Albert Camus.

What had gone into the making of this son of a Mandarin who also is a renowned Francophile? After graduating from the college Quoc Hoc in Hue, the best school in the country, he fought in the jungle against the French and the Americans, and now, for over twenty years, he has been at the head of a regime that is more repressive than any previous. But somewhat intimidated by his multitude of advisors, I didn't have the courage to ask that question.

Dong didn't address the question of attending the Synod of Bishops in Rome: "We regret that we cannot guarantee your safety abroad."

All other issues were also systematically rejected.

After ten minutes, Van Dong rose and bowed. "I beg your pardon, but I have to attend another meeting. I wish you every success." On the way out the Prime Minister added, "Don't hesitate to contact me if you have other questions."

We were bemused.

"Why didn't you speak about the suffering of the Christians?" I asked Dien.

For the first time since I have known him, he thundered, "Do you want to make my life impossible? That I suffer the same fate as Nguyen Van Thuan?"

Thinking of "my" former rector of the seminary, the music of the *Ninth Symphony* of Ludwig van Beethoven sounded again in my ears.

It was a sad return journey. The Archbishop had forgotten how to laugh. After having been cross-examined for four months, he was now publicly humiliated. Retreating into his office he became very silent.

Meanwhile, I represented the Archdiocese at meetings of the Fatherland Front. These meetings of the umbrella organization of the Communist associations started by singing the song *Ten Thousand Years*. That hymn wishes Ho Chi Minh longevity. When singing the refrain, the participants waved their hands in the air.

I observed this artificial enthusiasm with arms crossed. When someone scolded me, I answered, "Nothing in this world lives for ten thousand years. Am I correct in saying that Mr. Minh died in 1969?"

"Hmm, do you want me to carry your suitcase?" asked Kien.

I shook my head. "It is not heavy. There are no straitjackets or handcuffs in it."

The Lieutenant Colonel remained silent. He knew that at this early hour the slightest reaction could lead to a litany of complaints. He went into the kitchen, took a cup of coffee, and read the newspaper of the Fatherland Front.

"I've come for my Last Supper," I said when I wandered into the kitchen. On the front page I saw a picture of Vice President Ha Van Nui. Drool ran out of that man's mouth. The headline inferred that he had exchanged experiences about religion and ethnicity in Laos.

"What's going on? The Fatherland Front is also interested in religion?"

Because there was no reaction from him, I went a step further. "Shall I tell you something you don't know yet?"

This time he looked up.

"In April 1977, when you were still in elementary school learning about Marxism-Leninism, Archbishop Nguyen Kim Dien denounced the treatment of Catholics as second-class citizens at a meeting of the Fatherland Front. As the Director of the seminary, he and I distributed hundreds of copies of the text at home and abroad, and we disappeared behind bars. I got twenty years."

Kien put down his newspaper. "Hmm, and how many have you actually done?"

"Four months. Thanks to international protests after the admission of Vietnam to the United Nations, I was released on Christmas Eve. Although free, I was under house arrest in Doc So parish, and since that time, I have been forbidden to say Mass and preach."

Shaking his head, Kien plunged his head into the newspaper.

My mind travels back to Doc So. In 1978 I headed a small, close-knit, but traumatized parish.

"What has happened over here?"

"Leave the past behind," advised the oldest man of the village.

"Why do so many parishioners visit my predecessor's tomb every day?"

"He was a just man who cared for young people and the poor."

"What happened to him?"

"It's better that you don't know."

I gave the man a steely gaze. "I shall literally follow in his footsteps."

At first the man looks surprised but then he bowed his head. "The Viet Cong buried him alive in 1968."

"I don't think that the communists will dare to do that a second time," I said.

I saw a shy smile appear on his face.

"Tomorrow I hope to meet many people in order to clean up the parish hall," I said at the end of the evening prayer service. "We will create a study area. I personally, and others too, I hope, will also guide young people who have learning difficulties. We'll also have a recreation room where one can play chess and dominos. There'll be a ping-pong table next week. And then we'll organize a competition." There were spontaneous applause.

Afterwards, the communist mayor who was sitting in the first row approached me. "Congratulations. Our village needs people who take initiatives. And why shouldn't we work together? The municipality will create a farmers; cooperative association. Can you urge the farmers to join the association?"

"It looks like a valuable idea," I replied. "But I am not a farmer and everyone should decide whether to join or not join the association. Isn't Vietnam a free country?" Without saying another word he slinked off.

The next Saturday I directed the parishioners: "Tomorrow morning, take your pick-axe and your hoe and follow me after Mass." Together we cultivated the confiscated land of the Church, although we were offered a smaller lot, by way of compensation, that was less fertile and further away.

The next day, while I was playing dominos in the parish house with some young people, the major called me to account.

"Ly?"

Impassive, I kept on playing.

My neighbor said, "There is no Ly here, only Father Ly."

The major repeated, "I want to talk to the Father for a while." Immediately he exploded, "What gives you the right to farm government land?"

"Then answer the letter I sent you three weeks ago," I reacted. "Silence means consent. We could not wait any longer because the planting season has already started. And please excuse me, my playing partners expect me to play now."

My peaceful struggle for religious freedom began in Doc So. I never asked for permission for my activities, nor did I ever draw up a list of the names of the participants in the Masses and the Bible classes.

In my first manifesto, *Seven Just and Reasonable Points*, I listed the violations of human rights and listed the measures that restrict religious freedom. But how could I publish it? My colleague Phan Van Loi gave me a copy to the international human rights organizations. And Thi Hieu, my older sister, who remained unmarried and who visited me often with my parents, brought me an old loudspeaker from our former parish.

"That's the most useful gift I've ever received," I exclaimed with pleasure.

I hung that loudspeaker in the steeple of the church, and I myself read the text of the Manifesto through a microphone. Father didn't say one word, but he was beaming.

In this manner, I also broadcasted the Vietnamese programs of *Radio Veritas*, a Catholic radio station in the Philippines.

I continued to challenge Kien and asked, "What do you know about me?"

I loved to sow doubt in the mind of my head guard.

"From 1992 and after nine years in the camps, I was again placed under house arrest in the Archbishop's Palace where we are now."

Kien looked up.

"Don't look so surprised! Here I wrote the *Ten Point Program*, my indictment against the harmful effects of religious politics. Without being noticed, my colleague Van Loi, who visited me as recently as yesterday, managed to distribute hundreds of copies. Your intelligence network never knew this. There is no shortage of secret agents; getting them to work together is apparently impossible."

"You, with your manifestos and letters! What have you achieved? Nothing!"

"Religious freedom is crucial to every society. For that I will continue to fight my whole life."

"You, always with your faith." Kien makes a disposable gesture.

"You really don't want to understand it! Believing is about the call of God, and not that of Marx. The government wants to reconcile obedience to God and love of socialism. However, the more you force the faithful, the less they have sympathy for the hideous tyranny that you impose on their thoughts." I continued in a higher gear. "In addition, your words have no value whatsoever. The only words that can mean anything are those of the Secretary General of the Communist Party and the Prime Minister."

"Ah, don't think that they care about your writings!" laughed Kien. "Our country has other fish to fry with the village leaders than to take account of worldly ideas of erring priests."

Undaunted, I went on. "Why do I have to return to Nam Ha? Why was I exiled to Nguyet Bieu after I had written my *Ten Points Program*? Do you know what one of your bosses said in order to prevent the contamination of other priests? You are afraid. Yes afraid, because the authenticity of our faith threatens your corrupt regime."

Kien hid his face behind his newspaper.

I remember Nguyet Bieu; after Doc So, it was the second remote parish that I was assigned to as punishment. Starting in 1994, I was the successor of my other colleague and dissident, Huu Giai, over there.

"Your parish has less than a hundred believers," said Giai. "Because your pastoral mission is limited, you still have plenty of time. Why don't you teach? You speak different languages and have musical talent. And who in this country has such a knowledge of astronomy? In this region no training or specific education is offered. The only thing you find here are Communists stationed at the front and rear of the house and near your bedroom"

"You and your humor" I laughed.

I didn't think his idea crazy. "I accompanied young people with learning lag in Doc So, but I've never taught. Maybe I'm too hot-tempered? Because when I teach, I'll do it my way."

"Try it," said Giai encouragingly.

Many people showed up for my first French lesson. With the help of some parishioners, the offer was quickly extended to English, and music. People even came from Hanoi and Ho Chi Minh City, the former Saigon, to attend the course on astronomy.

I demanded full attention of the participants. Whoever was inattentive was expelled from the course after the first warning. The courses were free. I just asked for a small contribution for electricity. And those who didn't have money paid nothing.

At Nguyet Bieu, my interest in technology prompted me also to use a computer. But as they had quickly understood the potential danger, the authorities interfered and hampered the possible sale of computer equipment parts. Friends who had fled Vietnam and who lived in the United States sent me parts by mail. And tourists gave me packages. "Fragile" was written on the package above the symbol of a glass. With a manual in my hand, I patiently assembled my first computer and then a second, followed by a third. I also taught beginners how to use computers. But my priority went to the children of the poorest families.

Van Loi later helped me to establish a connection to the Internet. We kept this secret, because I sensed the enormous potential of this media. For the first time we were able to spread our ideas worldwide without being confronted with Communist censorship. What a revelation! I felt that the Internet would become the most powerful tool in my peaceful struggle for freedom. In anticipation of the use of our "secret weapon," we continued the use of the traditional "fighting methods." So in the year 2000, I hooked up the slogan "*Religious Freedom or Death*" to the church tower of Nguyet Bieu.

At five to six, I heard the chapel bell. Some retired colleagues shuffled to the chapel.

Kien got up. Since I received amnesty at *Tet* 2005, he is my inseparable shadow. However, he is the first Head Guard to have lasted longer than three months. He has become calmer in the last year, probably due to his Zen meditation exercises, but he doesn't speak about that for fear of losing his job. Last year, he was promoted from Major to Lieutenant Colonel. And there are those who wonder what good can come from a dissident priest! Despite our differences of views, a bond has grown between us. It seems we are destined for each other. I guess he will be there when I'm on my deathbed.

"Err, your wheelchair?" he asked.

I made a dismissive gesture. "In the Gospel of St. John we read, 'When you are young, you put on your own belt and walk where you like; but when you grow old, you will stretch out your hands, and somebody else will put a belt around you and take you where you would rather not go.' I don't feel old. My spirit is alive and well."

3

6:00 a.m.

"When I opened the sliding side door of the ambulance, the driver didn't move an inch. I climbed painfully aboard and clung to Kien when I tried to lie down. He put my legs straight.

With a sigh, a nurse wriggled in with a wicker basket and my walker.

"Good morning," she said gruffly. "Nurse Ngoc. I must accompany you. And with a sick priest on board. That's all I know."

It looked that she stood up with her wrong leg.

"Ah! You bring the provisions," said Kien.

"Why a nurse?" I was thinking by myself. "What could she possibly do should I suffer another stroke?"

Because of our travel bags, the space was very cramped. The metal folding seats were especially uncomfortable. I remembered last year's journey. Then we had to face the ordeal of sections of bad roads at the beginning of the journey; now they would come at the end of the journey. Anyway, this trip was to be a terrible ordeal for my poor body.

Similarly during the outward journey, we had little trouble with the driver. All he could do was mumble a few sounds that were like "yes" or "no."

Installed at his side, Phuc enjoyed his position of strength. He caressed the barrel of his gun. Did he think that I would want to escape? Without my walker, I couldn't even take two steps.

When Kien gave the signal to leave, Phuc indicated that I must be tied up. "These are orders." He produced the letter from a senior government official in Hanoi.

I protested. "I will not be put on a leash," and I turned to Kien. "You want to turn everyone into slaves. If Phuc could make decisions here, he would even put a muzzle on me. Because that's the goal—to silence me."

The Lieutenant Colonel, who was now under attack on both sides, raised his voice. "Shut up! I am the boss here, Phuc. The journey is already difficult enough. Ly will not be tied up."

Then he turned to me. "As for you, you're exaggerating things again. I've never silenced you."

"The 1.2 million employees of the Secret Service are spying on everyone in every city, every village, every street, and every house. Anyone whose head sticks out of the field is arrested." I gasped for breath. "Besides, the government sins against the Confucian tradition."

Kien pricked up his ears, for he had never heard this argument. "Confucius? What has the Chinese thinker and philosopher to do with the governance of our country? He lived 2,500 years ago."

"Following the example of Confucius, the communist propaganda cultivates the combination of talent and virtue and emphasizes the values of incorruptibility, moral leadership, and effective management every day on TV and in the newspapers. Yet our leaders are common bandits, and this country of ours is rotten to the bone. But you don't see that on TV."

Ngoc was stunned. "What's wrong with watching the seven-o'clock news? I watch every night at it. So I'm well informed about what's happening in our country. And why would I be dissatisfied? I'm happy. Last month, I was able to buy a moped for my son. Five years ago that was unthinkable."

Kien and Phuc nodded in agreement and the driver agreed with a buzzing sound.

"I'm talking about freedom. Our country only guarantees human rights on paper, because over and above everything and everyone sits the government with the Communist Party, the top of the hierarchy. They are untouchable and can get away with anything. What a farce!"

Suddenly it was quiet inside the car. The ambulance had to execute a difficult maneuver when it left the Palace of the Archbishop. We needed to drive onto the boulevard in the opposite direction. The danger didn't come from cyclists and rickshaws but from hundreds of scooters. When we finally managed to cross the road, a cacophony of horns and bells erupted.

I looked at the steeple of the chapel. My thoughts turned to my colleagues who were celebrating Mass. To unite myself with them, I took out my breviary; the now-battered copy that I got during my ordination remains my anchor.

I looked at the annotation made last night in the chapel. The first reading of the Mass for the coming weekend comes from Chapter 40 of the Book of Isaiah.

> Comfort my people, says your God.
> Speak tenderly to Jerusalem, and proclaim to her
> That her hard service has been completed.

It's been years since I had last read that text. The prophet Isaiah not only announces the end of exile, but also predicted that Yahweh himself will guide the return of the exiles.

> See, the Sovereign Lord comes with power.
> And he rules with a mighty arm.
> He tends his flock like a shepherd.

These words were written 2,700 years ago and are still relevant!

"No, our fight is not in vain," I convinced myself. "We will turn the tide! One day Vietnam will be freed from the Communist yoke. The question is not whether that will happen, but when."

I kissed the text of Isaiah and pressed it against my heart.

Nurse Ngoc pointed to the Central Hospital. "My father died there in 1987," she sighed.

"What happened to him?"

"A long illness." The tone of her voice betrayed the fact that his death continued to affect her. "First, he lived in the jungle during the war. And then he was deployed in the occupation of Cambodia. His health was broken."

"You have a Tonkin accent?"

"I was born in Vinh."

"Then you shouldn't worry. As a North Vietnamese and with a war hero in the family, your children will receive priority in the allocation of a scholarship and a place at the best colleges and universities. And later they can go to work for the government or a state-owned company. However, I advise you to become a member of the Communist Party, if you haven't already got your party card."

Ngoc shook her head.

"Such a card makes your life a lot easier. My guards can give you all the information about it."

Kien and Phuc looked at each other in despair, but remained silent.

"Another piece of good advice; always obey your bosses. For anyone who steps outside the line, there is the Rule of Three Generations. You not only put your own future at stake, but also that of your mother, your husband, and your children. They will be banished from school, their job will be taken from them, or access to health care denied."

Frightened, the nurse didn't know how to react.

"However, I have one consolation: Communism will self-destruct!"

At the traffic lights my words were drowned out by the decibels of the young guys on their scooters, so I repeated in a loud voice: "There will be no external attack. Communism will destroy itself."

"What are you saying now?" Ngoc exclaimed.

"Communism bears all the elements of self-destruction in itself. Atheism, materialism, hatred, violence combined with corruption and deception reinforce an already negative spiral. Only harsh repression manages to temporarily keep up appearances. But this cocktail is ultimately fatal. The large yellow star surrounded by a red field on the Vietnamese flag will soon be replaced by a shooting star."

Phuc threw a tantrum. "Damn it! Don't mock the symbol of our country."

I grinned.

We drove across the Perfume River, parallel to the citadel. I cast a last look at the impressive complex where I spent much of my free time on Sunday afternoons. And it must be said: it has been beautifully restored in recent years. I don't suspect the Communists have any interest in history or culture, but each year millions of tourists visit the Imperial City and that yields a lot of money.

We turned right, onto Main Road Number 1. At the Kim Long exit are the homes of former mandarins of the emperor. They are now inhabited by party officials. And on the horizon we see the seven-story Thien Mu Pagoda, once a hotbed of resistance against the French colonial power and the regime of President Ngo Dinh Diem. Monk Thich Quang Duc went from there in June 1963 to Saigon to set himself on fire.

"There," Ngoc pointed out a bit further. "My husband works in that factory."

To my surprise, I noticed a lot of construction activity from all sides.

"Why so quiet?" said Kien, who noticed my surprise. "Shall I refresh your memory? Since 1986, Vietnam has experienced economic growth of 7% each year. Or is that not permitted?"

"You know very well that the planned economy was replaced by capitalism because the occupation of Cambodia brought our country to the edge of the abyss."

Ngoc, who was certainly thinking of her father, listened intently.

"The *doi moi*, that infamous political reform, proves that this regime has no legitimacy at all. Marx and Lenin would turn in their graves if they were to see that their ideals were transformed into crass financial gain."

"Vietnam has only introduced free market economy, not capitalism," Kien defended himself.

I tried to set him straight: "What's the difference? What?"

Kien, who found it hard to invent a response, changed the topic immediately. "Poverty has decreased dramatically. Do you agree? You must be pleased as a friend of the poor."

For the first time today I couldn't contradict him. "Of course, I applaud the reduction in poverty." But after some thought I added that his triumphalism seemed totally inappropriate to me.

"Why then? Isn't that a major achievement of the government?"

"There would hardly be any poor people in Vietnam," I told him a little later, "because our country should have become an Asian Tiger like Singapore or South Korea." I shook my head. "But that will never happen."

"Because the Reverend knows everything better?"

"No, because the authorities don't conduct a policy against poverty. This decrease is only a side effect of the general increase in prosperity. Our political leaders have only one thing in mind: filling their own pockets. Name me one Communist government that is committed to fighting poverty."

No reply.

"Name just one!"

Throughout my life, I have always given priority to the less fortunate. I was still in the seminary when, during the holidays of 1968, I did an internship in Saigon with six worker-priests. Inspired by the spirituality of the French mystic and priest Charles de Foucauld, we lived in a mud house in the middle of a slum.

I sought no career but wanted to put my life completely in tune with the Gospel and be a humble servant close to the poor. I also wanted make the dream come true of Monsignor Van Thuan; all humans are family, as expressed in Beethoven's vision of the *Ninth Symphony*. And I made a living out of the itinerant sale of goods. Anything I earned I shared with the poor. I drew my inner strength from reading the Bible and praying.

One day during a police check I didn't have my papers on me, and I was sent to the recruitment centre of the South Vietnamese army. What a nightmare! I had to learn to shoot a gun. After intervention by my brother Nguyen Tri, who worked for the State Security, I was released.

On the motorway, heavily loaded trucks overtake us at high speed.

"It is important for your future and that of your children to work towards more freedom," I tried to convince Ngoc once again.

She shrugged.

"I know a story you can tell at home," I challenged her because I felt that she wasn't indifferent to what I said.

"What would that be?"

"In 2001, the new party leader, Nong Duc Manh, who is, as you know the illegitimate son of Ho Chi Minh, cracked down on dissidents. And do you know who was the first to be put behind bars?"

"You?"

"You guessed it!"

Unexpectedly, Kien intervened. "Ah! The Reverend forgot to say is that there was a good reason for this. He had sent two slanderous testimonies to the U.S. Congress in which he ridiculed our very moderate religious policy."

"Moderate?" I reacted outraged. "Why do identity cards mention one's religious preference? Why does the state appoint the priests and the bishops? Why are seized church properties not returned? And the religious prisoners not released?"

Nostalgically I remembered how, with the help of Phan Van Loi, I succeeded in sending my documents to the United States via email. To the frustration of the Secret Service that continually guarded me, we used the Internet as our "secret weapon" for the first time.

"Did you at least read these testimonies?" I challenged Kien. "Because they contained a correct and complete image of the religious situation in our country."

"Your baseless slander completely distorted the facts. It was a slap in the face to all Vietnamese."

"So you haven't read my documents. You only know the caricature that has appeared in the press. These texts were well and truly available on the Internet, but because of government censorship, not many people in Vietnam could read them."

Kien took a thick folder with documents out of his bag. A moment later he showed us an article entitled *A Snake in our Midst*. "Listen to what the editor of the most influential newspaper in our country writes. 'The testimony of Nguyen Van Ly will only benefit the small group of overseas Vietnamese who want to undermine the country for their personal interest.' What do you think of that, nurse?"

"That the Communists have a well-oiled propaganda machine," I replied in her place.

Ngoc didn't know what had hit her.

"Or do you want me to quote a colleague of the Reverend?" Kien continued.

I protested, but he elevated his voice.

"A priest should teach religion and help people put the biblical texts into practice, but he shouldn't engage in economics and politics. Van Ly is a saboteur of the Christian religion. He should be punished by the Archbishop and the government."

"Where do you get all this nonsense?"

"And here's another colleague, 'Everyone knows the evil acts of Van Ly, and they want him to be punished severely. Everyone is surprised that . . .'"

I tried to intervene again, but my effort was in vain. Kien continued, "Everyone is surprised that he still behaves so provocatively, ignores the law, and spreads messages that encourage Catholics to revolt. He has never shown any sign of remorse or of self-correction. Shouldn't the authorities urgently prevent the spread of his poisonous ideas?'"

Kien was on a roll. "Do you know on top of that that, the Reverend advised the U.S. Congress not to approve the trade agreement with this country? And this guy calls himself a Vietnamese! How dare you!"

He put down his file and waved both arms. "Why do the Americans interfere in our country? The Vietnamese government would do well to expose once and for all the atrocities committed by the Americans in the prison camp of Guantanamo. Ah, that would make some noise!"

I tried in vain to intervene.

"And that's not all. In 2001, he also wrote a series of summons to the government. I saw one of these texts. Do you know what he did? The Reverend had changed the slogan '*Independence—Freedom—Happiness*' on the official letterhead to '*Lack of Independence—Loss of Freedom—No Happiness*.' You are a disgrace to our country!"

"Damn it. A shame. Damn shame," agreed Phuc.

"Shame." Emitting a deep sigh that resembled a laugh, the driver approved his words.

"Where does this anger come from?" I said and turned to Ngoc. "It is the truth that hurts."

Nineteen summonses. Despite my arrest, my sister Thi Hieu, when she stayed with me, and parishioners that I could trust 100 percent were able to bring them, one after the other, surreptitiously to Phan Van Loi, who put them on the Internet. Because the government did not understand how that was possible, I got two extra guards. But my smuggling route was not detected.

The first victim of the authorities' wrath was Lars Rise, a member of the Norwegian Parliament. In April 2001, he and hundreds of worshipers attending an evening service in the church met me afterwards in the sacristy. Twenty minutes later my assistant reported that the police had surrounded the church. A few minutes later the police broke open the locked church door. Rise and his entourage were arrested and interrogated until three o'clock. The interrogation continued through the morning until shortly after noon, when the delegation was put on a plane in Da Nang to Ho Chi Minh City and expelled from the country.

A month later, I was arrested by six hundred agents. The police actually wanted to be greater in number than the parishioners. These were simple farmers who, every morning at half past four, recited their rosary and then attended Holy Mass.

"More and more soldiers have surrounded the church," parishioners whispered in my ear. But I started celebrating Mass without any fear. Accompanied by the organist, I heartily sang the opening hymn:

> We carry your Word,
> It touches us, it drives us.

I saw hordes of soldiers invading the church via the two aisles. They headed straight for the altar. While the organist continued his singing, the parishioners screamed, "Save our priest!"

Some rushed forward to protect me, but they were beaten with truncheons and electric batons. It was the first time I had seen this type of weapon. An elderly woman who had already stood watch all night was thrown on the floor and kicked. And my faithful servant, a seventy-year-old man who stood guard at the church for one hundred days, was manhandled with the electric batons. To my consternation his body was covered with bloodstains. He groaned in pain.

A special unit grabbed me by the collar and dragged me out of the church.

The organ music turned into a cacophony, because the organist was also beaten up.

All the parishioners were forcibly placed against the outside walls of the church. Whoever moved was beaten up.

"What happened afterwards?" asked Ngoc curiously, looking very pale now. "So much violence. Why was that necessary?"

I stared at Kien. His anger seemed to have subsided.

The next day, two hundred parishioners visited the headquarters of the Communist Party. When asked by the police where they were going, the children who marched at the front said, "We are searching for our priest. Bring him back!"

"You drivel on, man," intervened Phuc. "Damn it. How do you know that? You were arrested!"

"Dozens of witnesses told me on the same story later. The hastily summoned police reinforcements again scattered the parishioners beating them with electric batons. Meanwhile, the protesters shouted 'Down with the regime of terror' and 'Religious Freedom or Death.'"

A young woman stepped forward and asked, "Where did you hide him? If you have murdered him and secretly buried him then at least bring us his body."

When the police threatened to shoot her, she shouted, "I'm ready to die! Shoot me!"

Ngoc had tears in her eyes, but Phuc intervened with his hearty laugh. "Don't believe too damn much of what the pastor says. He is a champion of exaggeration."

"There is evidence," I replied indignantly. "The police filmed everything. Everyone had to take off his or her straw hat. These images were later used as evidence against the protesters."

It was not the first time that I was violently arrested. In 1983, when officers surrounded the parish and the church of Doc So, I mobilized my parishioners through the loudspeaker on the church tower. Dozens of parishioners spent the night in the rectory. By candlelight, prayer forged a close bond. Those who came to join us the next day brought us food and drink. We shared everything we had. Given the sheer number of participants, the police did not dare to intervene immediately.

In a letter to the Communist Party, I promised to stop my activities provided I received an answer to my first manifesto, *Seven Just and Reasonable Points*, that I had sent five years earlier.

As there was no reply from the government, I distributed my second manifesto *My Final and Ultimate Position* with the help of Van Loi. The announcement that I would continue my battle until I got satisfaction on all issues had resulted in a tripling of the number of officers stationed around the rectory and church. Although supply of food and drink was disrupted, dozens of believers, and some of them Buddhists, stood by my side.

A few weeks later, the authorities decided to intervene anyway. After the first Mass, 300 armed soldiers quickly and violently forced their way in between the parishioners. An officer attacked me on the back with a baton and struck me until I lost consciousness.

That same day, Amnesty International adopted me as a prisoner of conscience, a status that I have had now for almost thirty years.

We drove past a sign with the town name "Quang Tri." In the distance I see the remnants of the Citadel—a mini-version of the Imperial Palace in Hue. But the citadel was also severely damaged during the war.

In Quang Tri, I attended lower secondary school from 1960 to 1963.

A little further on, an arrow indicated the route of La Vang.

"Stop!" I shouted. "I have to go to the toilet urgently."

Surprised, Kien gave the order to leave the Main Road.

The ambulance stopped on the side of the road.

"No, a toilet," I repeated. "Four kilometers further down is the cafeteria of the place of pilgrimage."

Kien's look revealed that he suspected I was up to something, but he agreed.

Beaming with happiness, I clambered out of the car. Next to the statue of Our Lady, I saw the new basilica that had been consecrated in January 2011. Finally, it had happened! Pope John Paul II dreamed of completing the reconstruction of the basilica in 1998 for the bicentenary of the apparitions. Better late than never.

"The cafeteria is closed," said the cleaning woman. When I showed her the little cross on my shirt, she let me in.

"Why did you absolutely want to stop here?" Kien was leaning against the wall while I was washing my hands.

"I used to live two kilometers further down."

My thoughts went back to 1955.

The French defeat at Dien Bien Phu announced the end of colonial rule, and the Geneva Conference that followed divided the country. North Vietnam got a communist government led by Ho Chi Minh, and South Vietnam remained within the Western sphere of influence. Anyone who wanted could, nevertheless, move. A million people left the North, mostly Catholics, among whom all the people of my hometown Ba Ngoat, on the territory of the municipality Ho Xa.

Although I was only eight years old at the time, I remember that day like it was yesterday.

Waving his hands around the priest gave instructions. "No furniture. Take only clothes and food."

My sister Thi Hieu helped me stuff all my things into my hard-shell suitcase; we both sat on top of the suitcase to force it shut.

"When will we go back home?" I asked the priest.

"It won't be long. We'll have elections in two years' time. Then the country will be reunited again." His face lit up with a big smile.

"I don't believe a word of it," grumbled my father later on. "The Communists don't accept any compromise. There will be no elections."

Seven trucks of the French army rumbled through the village.

"We were promised twelve," protested the priest.

"We do what we can," the French soldier said. "We are trying to help everyone . . ."

"All men over the age of twelve will walk," announced the pastor. "We'll meet in Quang Tri."

When our truck moved forward jerkily on the dirt road, grandmother started to weep softly. Mama comforted her. I cast a last glance at my birthplace. Suddenly it dawned on me that the toy car I got from my brother Nguyen San was still under my bed. I started to cry.

"The door isn't locked, Mom," I shouted. "What if thieves steal my car?"

She smiled. "No house is locked and who would take your car now? Next year we will be back here."

"But Papa says . . ."

Mom held me against her. I hardly dared move for fear of breaking the spell of her embrace.

I woke up in a refugee camp near Quang Tri. We slept in tents. Volunteers were struggling to make our stay as pleasant as possible. Mom and Dad lived in joyful expectation. South Vietnamese President Diem had, indeed, promised to give a plot of fertile land to each refugee.

A year later, six new villages sprang up in the hilly forest surrounding the shrine of La Vang. We moved to the centre of La Vang. Around the new church volunteers of an American aid organization built prefabricated houses. They wore blue T-shirts with the letters CRS.

As the crow flies, our former village was barely forty kilometers further north. However, life was not like before. As the land was less fertile, we also had less to eat.

"When are we going back, Papa?"

Silence.

"Finish your plate," ordered my sister Hieu.

"Does that village still exist?" Kien asked. "I never heard you speak about it."

My breath gasps. "The Communist Easter Offensive of 1972 razed the whole area."

I got a lump in my throat. "My two adopted brothers died in combat over there. They fought in the South Vietnamese army. Finding work was difficult and the barracks were nearby. Nguyen Van Toan left a woman with seven children. The war has heavily marked our family." I hesitated for a moment. "Yours as well?"

Kien turned his head away.

"Your place is not in the seminary now. Come home immediately. The whole village must move today." I heard panic in the voice of my father.

Of course I had heard the morning news. The North Vietnamese army had launched an offensive in the province of Quang Tri. But did everything really happen so quickly? Or did the South Vietnamese radio give a distorted picture of the situation?

I took the bus, but I was the only passenger. The refugee flow in the opposite direction made the journey difficult. It was not until four hours later that I arrived at La Vang.

The truck engines of the South Vietnamese army were running while three hundred villagers were boarding the trucks with all their possessions. The memories of our first flight, seventeen years earlier, resurfaced.

There was, indeed, a sense of urgency. Bombs were coming perilously close. The target was the South Vietnamese military camp that was only five kilometers away as the crow flies. I felt the earth vibrating.

"We should run to Hue as quickly as possible," I advised the priest.

We drove away from the war zone and approached the old imperial capital at nightfall.

The director of the parish school near the airport of Hue, where I taught catechism, allowed us to spend the evening there. That same night the priest gave me a ride to the airport. We were lucky. The next morning we could board one of the South Vietnamese army's C-130s. This aircraft had to fetch equipment in the military camp of Bien Hoa, north of Saigon.

The women and children sat in hammocks along the fuselage of the aircraft. The men stood in the middle with their luggage. I saw happy faces, but fear hid underneath. What would the future hold? Could the South Vietnamese army hold out now that the Americans were about to leave Vietnam?

Upon arrival in Bien Hoa, we learned that we had narrowly escaped hell. "The region of La Vang was completely destroyed," announced the radio reporter.

At first, we stayed temporarily in a tent camp on a soccer field. Later we moved to a small village, but its serenity was unfortunately marred with night raids by the Viet Cong.

In our search for a definitive solution we came across a site that was owned by the Ministry of Agriculture.

"Do you know anyone at the Department of Agriculture?" I asked Nguyen San.

"I'll call you back."

That same day we had a meeting with a senior official. The man hailed from Quang Tri and he was willing to listen to our request.

"Five minutes. I will put the question to the minister."

We kneeled in silence and began to pray. Every minute seemed like an eternity. Our pastor with his sore knee was gritting his teeth.

When he came back into the office, the official was scared out of his wits, seeing us kneeling in prayer. But he had good news. We would get the approval in due course with the stamp and signature of the Minister.

"Our prayer was heard!" the priest triumphed.

The area on the edge of the jungle was overgrown with trees and bamboo bushes. I drew a map with a checkerboard pattern around the church, the school, and the market. Each family was allocated an equal plot of land. We called our new home Quang Bien—a contraction of the place Quang Tri, the province from which we came, and the city of Bien Hoa. With great enthusiasm and the solidarity of the Catholic parishes in the neighborhood, we created a new village.

"We have to go now," Kien said.

I looked up. "Thanks." I appreciate that you've allowed me this stop over. La Vang is close to my heart."

Kien offered me his arm when we left.

"Compared to my previous head guards you at least show me some respect," I told him straight from my heart. "I cannot tell you this in the presence of others, but I appreciate the way you perform your job."

Kien looked surprised.

"Respect. Remember that word. Only mutual respect will ensure that we will grow into a more peaceful society."

4

9:00 a.m.

"What is so special about that place?" Ngoc asked curiously.

"Curiosity is feminine," I smiled. "La Vang was the most popular Catholic pilgrimage site of Asia. The Blessed Virgin appeared there several times."

"Oh, and you believe that?" Kien sneered.

I looked him straight in the eyes. Mutually, we felt that in this new "war of words," everyone creeped to his familiar position again.

"Of course," I answered self-assured.

Undaunted by the loud laugh of Phuc and the grunts of the driver I continued, "Many people have doubts in this regard, but my belief does not depend on those appearances. They are not the core of my faith."

"So it's possible they are just fantasies?"

"There is indeed no scientific evidence."

Phuc intervened with his hearty laugh.

"Well now, you couldn't convince me at all," Kien intervened. "Give me an explanation! You always know an answer to every question."

"One believes with one's heart rather than with one's mind. I found that many pilgrims find inner peace in La Vang. The visit to La Vang makes them stronger. The attraction of La Vang is illustrated by the fact that Christians from other countries also used to come here. This is a privileged place where the world and the divine touch one another."

"I did not feel anything," Kien said. "I only saw the bricks of a church and large mushroom-shaped forms with a statue underneath."

"There is a dimension in life that we can't see with our senses."

Phuc laughed, "My senses are still working!"

"Do you know the answer to the important existential questions: Who are we? Where do we come from? Why do we have to suffer so much? And where are we heading to after our death?"

Phuc turned around and looked in front of him.

"So you don't know the answers. Knowing that something or somebody transcends us, religions provide an answer to those existential questions. We Christians believe in God. Buddhists, Hindus, Taoists, and others put their own interpretation on those issues. But ultimately it's about the same thing: giving sense and meaning to the transcendent, cosmic dimension or that which we cannot grab with both hands or understand with our logical mind."

Kien remained impassive while Ngoc was wiggling in her car seat.

"The belief in ghosts and the cult of the ancestors are other examples of this deep-rooted religious sense in every human being. When I'm talking to people, also to so-called nonbelievers, I note that deep in them a religious feeling is present, even without them knowing this because in our society the communist regime uses every available means to suppresses this feeling and it is shrouded by taboos. This explains why Nurse Ngoc has never been able to cope with her father's death."

Ngoc blushed a deep red.

I turned to her. "Do you believe in ghosts and the cult of the ancestors?"

As if rooted to the spot, Ngoc shyly nodded.

"Why would you be ashamed about your belief? The belief in spirits and ancestor worship is in the genes of every Vietnamese person. We Catholics also honor our ancestors because we are primarily Vietnamese."

I looked Kien straight in the eyes. "Only the Communists, as atheists, reject belief in anything. Is it true what I say?"

A honking truck startled me when we drove up Main Road Number 1.

For Kien, this was a signal to change the subject once again. "I'll return to the subject of the ancestors later. But I've never understood Catholicism in Vietnam. You don't worship ghosts but a single God. And until recently your celebrations were held in Latin, a language that no one understands. That is still at odds with how we Vietnamese are, isn't it? Or am I wrong? Explain to me the attraction of Catholicism in Vietnam. Why are one in ten Vietnamese people Catholic?"

Kien was so cunning! He never revealed his thoughts. And what was he hiding? However, his question touched the core reason for the Catholic presence in our country. Somewhat surprised, I tried to organize my thought.

"I'm listening," Kien said, sensing my hesitation.

"It's a long story," I sighed. "We should start at the beginning when the first Catholic missionaries arrived over here in the seventeenth century. They were successful with the poor fishermen and farmers through their radical application of the love of your fellow men and the principle of solidarity"

"Yet they lived in isolated enclaves?"

"That happened much later. But who knows that part of our history? This is not mentioned in the textbooks at school. These textbooks are all steeped in Marxist-Leninist ideology."

"What happened?" Ngoc asked. She was listening intently.

"After the unification of Vietnam in 1802, with French help, the emperors curtailed Western influences in fear of foreign domination. They surely feared a French domination of Vietnam. And since many French people were Catholics, the emperors considered the Vietnamese Catholics a "fifth column" of the French government. That was wholly unjustified, but the result was that a genocide took place: Catholics were murdered everywhere. The death toll reached up to a hundred thousand. Whole villages were wiped out, all the inhabitants murdered. People were slaughtered—not for what they had done, but only because they were Catholics."

I look Phuc straight in the eyes, but this time he didn't flinch.

"Hundred thousand?" Nurse Ngoc asked, appalled.

I nodded. "Because of the genocide, Catholics retreated to fortified enclaves in remote areas. My parish, Ba Ngoat, was situated in a region notorious for gangs of robbers. Anyway, French Emperor Napoleon III ordered the colonization of Vietnam."

"And then the *Can Vuong* took place, the insurgency of the supporters of the Emperor against the French occupying forces?" Kien said.

"Exactly. And who were their target population?"

"The French?" Ngoc said.

"Forget it. They had superior military power. Once again the Vietnamese Catholics were massacred. 40,000 were murdered. In my native village Ba Ngoat alone, 450 people lost their lives. Only old people, women, and children were spared."

The driver also was petrified.

"The history of the Vietnamese Catholics is drenched in blood. But as is usual in history, the blood of the martyrs is the seed for new converts."

We approach Dong Ha. The city was a hive of activity. I saw new industrial areas, and we drove past a railway line under construction. The border with Laos is just eighty kilometers away in the west. This is main gateway to the country that itself has no access to the sea.

I looked but saw no visible trace of the intense fighting that took place here until 1975. Fifteen kilometers further down we got on a ridge overlooking vast rice fields and the Ban Hai River at the height of the 17th latitude.

"It is here that the Americans built one command post next to another during the war. Look to the right," pointed Kien. "The post of Doc Mieu, which is still preserved."

Because the Main Road runs parallel to the historic Hien Luong Bridge, which is unused today, the traffic slowed down. Buses were lined up at this popular tourist attraction.

"For twenty years, this was the physical and psychological barrier between North and South," said Kien. "The original bridge was painted half red and half yellow."

A little further down one can visit a huge cemetery for North Vietnamese soldiers and Viet Cong fighters.

"My two uncles are buried here," said Ngoc almost in a whisper.

Kien didn't stir.

"Did you lose relatives during the war?" the nurse asked.

"Who didn't?" Kien was gritting his teeth.

Ngoc put her hand on his shoulder. "I feel that you're still affected by a tragic event that happened during the war," she said cautiously. "I'm not keen to know what that is. You can decide when the time is right to talk about this, but I'm sure talking will provide some relief. We don't talk enough about our feelings."

Because of the maternal tone in Ngoc's voice, Kien broke down. Tears rolled down his cheeks.

"My only daughter, Loan," said Kien with a lump in his throat. "She was a victim of Agent Orange . . . that dirty defoliant of the Americans . . . because my wife and child had eaten . . . contaminated food . . . her immune system was compromised . . . Loan is ten years old, but she looks like a child of five . . . She will never be able to walk . . . Her nervous system is affected . . . She lives in an institution in Da Nang."

His breath gasped. "As if that was not enough, my wife was diagnosed with cancer a few months ago." He raised his voice. "Every day I get up and go to sleep with the war . . . thanks to all the poison that the Americans sprayed over here!" His voice trembled. "150,000 . . . 150,000 children with abnormalities . . . The U.S. war veterans received compensation . . . We only got crumbs . . . I received five dollars after signing a statement in which I renounced any further claim." He put his right hand in the air. "Five dollars . . . it was that or nothing . . . Where is the justice? . . . What are all these international organizations for?"

I was deeply impressed by his spontaneous confession. This was the first time Kien had talked to me about that problem. "You're so right," I stammered. "You're the victim of unpunished immoral acts that have never been redressed. Nobody can approve of the misdeeds of the United States."

"And yet you have the same faith," said Kien on sharp tone, but still very emotional.

"Agent Orange has nothing to do with religion, but everything to do with irresponsible abuse of power. This is a crime against humanity that never has been punished. It's use today would no longer be possible."

"What does that change for me?" He swallowed his tears. "Now, my wife is . . . also . . . sentenced to death . . . Every day I 'm obsessed with this one question . . . What will happen to Loan . . . when I'm gone? . . . Who will take care of her? Who?"

"Your suffering touches me deeply. I will truly and sincerely pray for your daughter, your wife, and you yourself. I know this does not solve your problem, but when we feel that others help us by carrying our pain, we become stronger."

It became awfully quiet in the car.

"I feel perfectly what you feel," I continued. "You're just as broken as the nature we are now driving through. Quite the whole region remains infertile because of the use of pesticides and napalm. Look, on the ridges you can only see deformed pine trees. They are the silent witnesses to the horror that is almost unmatched in the history of mankind. They symbolize the suffering that plagues this region, this country, and many inhabitants.

My words were touching to the Lieutenant Colonel, who steadied his breath. "The American War was a war of attrition," sighed Kien. "General Giap, Chief of the North Vietnamese Forces, was convinced that the Americans, as previously the French, would retreat if the war lasted long enough. He continuously mobilized new soldiers because of the inequality of firepower. Thirteen communist fighters died for every American killed in combat."

Kien repeated his words: "Thirteen! What a huge loss of lives! The entire North Vietnamese population was mobilized."

Nurse Ngoc agreed. "While my father was in the army, my mother took his place in the factory. And although all my aunties were working in the fields, people in the North were starving. All the food was for the soldiers."

"It was indeed a strange war," I added. "The more hypermodern armaments the Americans supplied, the more the Viet Cong infiltrated South Vietnamese territory."

"As a child, I used the secret Ho Chi Minh Trail to go to Cu Chi, forty kilometers from the former capital Saigon. I crawled through the original tunnels that now have been enlarged for tourists. How ridiculous is that!"

"How did the trip go?" Ngoc wanted to know.

Probably for the first time ever Kien openly talked about what he had experienced. "I still remember the American bombings. My mother and I survived, but my father did not." He almost choked. "And," he continued after a short pause, "Do you now understand my natural aversion for your American friends?"

"The Americans are not my friends."

"Hello? Twice you have made defamatory statements before the American Congress?"

"I value the fact that Americans worldwide play a leading role in the struggle for enforcing human rights. These are essential for all forms of society. For who today still defends those rights? Certainly not your Chinese friends. Even Liu Xiaobo, who recently received the Nobel Peace Prize, will spend the next ten years in prison."

"Don't change the subject!" Kien snapped. "I wasn't talking about the Chinese, but about the Americans."

"All my life I have denounced the evils of the American army in Vietnam. However, there are two sides to this coin because Vietnam was where the USA and the Soviet Union were fighting their Cold War."

Kien interrupted me. "I see what you mean. You're going to blame the Soviets."

"I didn't say that. This war had nothing to do with Vietnam; it was all about the drive of the former superpowers to show who was the strongest. What I find most disgusting is that the Americans immediately continued the Cold War in Nicaragua, El Salvador, and Mozambique when they retreated from the Vietnamese impasse."

Kien who for the first time agreed with me, immediately interrupted me, "And this without bothering about the mess they left behind—one and a half million deaths and three million wounded. And on top of that, two million victims in the neighboring countries Laos and Cambodia."

"This time I thoroughly agree with you," I said. "I'll never forget the figures in the report I wrote for Monsignor Dien on the social breakdown of the country: ten million refugees, three million unemployed, one million widows, one million orphans, and hundreds of thousands war invalids and disabled people. Vietnam was one big ruin and was one of the poorest countries on earth."

Kien beamed. "The communists you despise have nevertheless succeeded in turning things back the right way up."

"Sorry," I interrupted him, "but that is . . ."

"Checkmate," Phuc triumphed. "Well done! He is in checkmate! Long live the communists!"

While Ngoc was laughing, the driver shouted a primal noise.

I shook my head, but I couldn't handle so much verbal aggression.

At a gas station I saw a signpost to Ho Xa. My native village Ba Ngoat was part of that municipality. This is where I was born on Sunday, August, 31, 1947—the youngest son in a family of five children. Although my parents were very poor, my parents adopted two homeless children.

My earliest childhood memories are marked by civil war against the French colonizers. Following the nocturnal attacks by the Viet Minh, the communist movement that resisted the French colonizers, our village was transformed into a fortress of clay. All men between eighteen and sixty years old were required to serve in the civic guard.

I was about three years old when gunshots woke me up. As we slept and lived in the same room, I snuggled up in my mother's arms, away from all the screaming and screeching. I dared not move.

Moments later, our neighbor and my best friend Truc stood crying in front of our door. My father lit a candle and opened the barricaded door. His legs trembling, Truc ran towards me. Panicking, his mother told her story.

The Viet Minh had abducted her husband and two members of the village council. Two other members who resisted were shot on the spot.

The next morning on the streets I saw the corpses of three Viet Minh soldiers. The earth around was impregnated with a reddish liquid. The dead were buried the same day. The whole village was in mourning.

A year later we were playing when we saw Truc's father limping into the village, leaning on a stick. Truc ran towards him, "Papa is back!" Both cried with happiness. Truc's father showed the scars of his torture. "Horrible," was the only word he managed to say. The stay in the camps had broken his health.

I always saw him lying in bed. When he died six years later, his family only managed to survive thanks to the existing solidarity. As brothers and sisters, we shared what little we had. What brought us together was our faith. Every day we met in the church at five o'clock in the morning for Mass and at six o'clock in the evening for the prayer service.

In our parish there was an ambiguous feeling towards the regular visit of French missionaries. According to my father, they had ties that were too close with the arrogant colonial rulers.

"He was particularly critical towards landowners and merchants who, without criticism, adopted the French language and culture. "A Vietnamese in a Western suit! What a farce! And what sort of Vietnamese drinks wine, rides a bicycle, and sends his children to a French school?" But his laughter had a bitter undertone as he looked with dismay at how the traditional society was eroding. He refused to accept the French laws because they ignored the local traditions. In family disputes, the *paterfamilias* and religious leaders no longer had the last word. In his eyes, the French law was just a tool of oppression, because all opponents disappeared behind bars for years without any trial. Dad refused consequently to learn French and did not use *quốc ngữ*, the modern Vietnamese writing system based on the Roman alphabet.

But not everyone shared his vision.

"You'll never change the world by taking radical positions or by turning back the clock," the priest would say when debating with my father. "Look at the positive side. Many French also are Christians. And what would the alternative be? Do you have more confidence in those godless communists?"

"I'll never be a lackey," my father replied. "Not of the French and certainly not of the communists. It is essential that our ancient culture, traditions, norms, and values are not lost. But who will defend them?"

With his common sense, he also denounced economic exploitation. "Our coal is exported to France, while our stores only offer expensive French products. And what justifies the French monopoly on the production and sale of not only alcohol and salt, but also addictive opium that is grown everywhere?"

Father saw with his own eyes how the farmers had become impoverished because of the marketing of the rice harvest that caused the prices to fall. Many people sold their land and went to work as cheap laborers in mines and rubber plantations. "The imperial ban on rice exports should never have been lifted, because it served to supply the regions where there was a shortage of rice and to build up reserves for the lean years."

Meter-high panels advertise attractive four- and five-star hotels. Everything must give way for tourism, the fastest growing industry in the country. The burned-out tanks that had still stood along the road last year were neatly removed.

A little further along the road is a sign advertising the Vinh Moc tunnels.

I shake my head. Vinh Moc. As a child I attended the elementary school over there. It was a small, insignificant village. Now each year, hundreds of thousands of tourists visit the tunnel complex that the villagers dug to protect themselves against the American bombing.

"I've been there once," Kien said. "It's impressive how hundreds of people survived all the American bombings in tunnels three floors below ground that they had dug with shovels, baskets and their bare hands. Everything was available there. For example, seventeen children were born in the makeshift infirmary."

"Knowing the Communists, the site will only show the 'good' side of the war, with the Viet Cong as the good guys and the Americans as the bad guys," I responded. "I've never read a single word about the massacres of the Viet Cong and all the evil that they've done. Woe to him who dares to touch this taboo."

We could have heard a pin drop in the car. I addressed Nurse Ngoc. "In war, there are no good or bad guys. Whoever takes up arms is guilty, regardless of whose side he is on."

Half an hour later, we entered Dong Hoi, the capital of the province Quang Binh. Razed to the ground several times during the war, the city has been beautifully rebuilt. Especially the promenade along the river looks beautiful. Here, too, construction is booming. The only visible reminder of the war is the tower of the Tam Toa Church. The rest of the building was destroyed by an American bombing in 1968. Under the tower, the faithful celebrated Mass every week until the local authorities banned it. In 2009, after protracted negotiations, fourteen priests with the support of the Bishop of Vinh ignored the ban. When the rumor circulated that the tower would be converted into a tourist office, the parishioners erected a cross and an altar near the tower. But police "cleansed" the area and arrested twelve demonstrators.

Since then, the atmosphere has been tense. The Party newspaper *Nhan Dan* recently unveiled the proposed development of a park, which would require demolition of the tower.

As we were caught in a traffic jam, for the first time I had the opportunity to see the tower up close. Trees are growing on the walls and on the bell tower. Crowd control barriers prevent anyone entering the area.

"I have to get gas," grumbled the driver, swerving into the gas station next to the church square.

For a moment I was allowed out of the car. Behind my walker, I hobbled up to the fences around the ruins. Despite the early hour, dozens of believers were already gathered there. Inside, police patrol with dogs. I saw that the cross and the altar had been destroyed and the terrain was overgrown with weeds. Hundreds of novena candles had been lit near the barriers. To my great surprise, these were beside the memorial stone of Han Mac Tu. This famous poet, who died in 1940 at the age of 28, was baptized here.

"He was ahead of his time," a bystander told me. "I've always enjoyed reading his poems. I teach in high school and found that many young people are crazy about his writings." He laughed. "Much more so than the material on Marxism and Leninism that is imposed on them and that many teachers don't want to teach anymore."

I remember the poetry of Han Mac Tu from my time in the seminary and know some of his tormented verses by heart.

"How is it, that seventy years after his death, this man still inspires so many people?"

"He was a Catholic but he also incorporated Buddhist thoughts and images in his poems. He symbolized the resistance to any form of religious oppression. And that resonates with young people."

To my surprise I heard a group of young people singing the *Song of Peace* by Kim Long in the distance.

> Lord, teach me to love and to serve God.
> Make me an instrument of your peace.
> Where there is hatred, let me sow love
> And learn to forgive
> And endure disease and oppression.

I hobbled towards them. The priest who accompanied the group noticed my cross and greeted me warmly.

"We come from Vinh."

Arms outstretched, he excitedly addressed the people at the crowd barrier. "Today, we make a pilgrimage to Dong Hoi. Why? Because it is the cradle of Catholicism in our country. It was here that in the seventeenth-century missionaries founded one of the first parishes. The Communists intend to transform this tower into a symbol of the American barbaric behavior during the war. To us, however, a church tower serves to call the faithful to worship. That's its only possible purpose. Therefore, we continue to peacefully demonstrate for the return of the tower and all confiscated church properties. In this time of Advent, we hope, as Christians, that justice will finally prevail in this country."

I heard someone calling my name. The young people were booing when Phuc grabbed me by the collar.

"Our weapons are candles and prayer," said the priest who saw that Kien and Phuc were about to escort me back to the car.

Using my walker, I held them back.

"One more minute!"

Kien motioned Phuc to release me.

I looked the priest right in the eyes.

"As religious people, we must speak on behalf of those who have no right to speak," the priest said. "We must proclaim the truth as Christ has always done, even if we are persecuted because of it."

The pastor turned to me. "I don't know the priest that you want to take away by force. However, I see in his eyes that he is a righteous man who defends the truth. Let's show him what love for fellow men means and kneel down in prayer for this persecuted priest."

I gratefully bowed and meekly followed Kien and Phuc who dragged me to the ambulance. Adrenaline raged through my body. Since the events of two years ago, I had heard nothing more about the tower of Dong Hoi, not even in the foreign newspapers that I read in Hue on the Internet. But one thing is certain: over here, the hatchet is not yet buried.

I looked one last time at the young people and their enthusiastic priest. I have to reconsider my opinion. There are still, indeed, priests and Christians who protest against the communist regime. They are the future of the Church and the country.

5

Noon

As we left the city of Dong Hoi in bumper-to-bumper traffic, the feeling of excitement that had overwhelmed me did not disappear. However, the excitement turned into a sensation of paralysis; it was as if I had lost all feeling in the right part of my body—face, arm, and leg—and I heard myself spouting gibberish.

"Nurse Ngoc!" Kien panicked. "Something serious is going on."

She dropped her magazine and slapped my face. "Show me your teeth!"

I hardly reacted.

"The right corner of his mouth doesn't hang down. I don't think he has suffered a stroke, but he seems to be confused." She took my blood pressure. "160 over 80. Much too high."

Meanwhile, untroubled by the events, Phuc and the driver were chatting.

"Shut up!" Kien gruffly ordered.

"You too, you better calm down," said Ngoc sternly. "Panic gets you nowhere. If his condition doesn't improve, we must return to the hospital in Dong Hoi immediately. But for now, we need to wait and see."

A few minutes later the oppressive feeling ebbed away. I breathed more calmly again. "I think . . . that . . . the danger has passed." My voice was still weak. "At my age . . . I don't seem . . . to be able to deal with . . . emotions."

Ngoc again took my blood pressure.

"140 over 70. Much better. You didn't suffer a stroke, so keep yourself calm," she ordered.

A relieved Kien wiped his forehead with his handkerchief.

Moments later, I felt better and asked, "Could you give me the small package that's in my bag?"

I'm curious to know what gift Van Loi gave me. The shape of the package reveals that there were two objects in it. Out came a CD of the *Ninth Symphony* by Ludwig van Beethoven by the Berlin Philharmonic conducted by Claudio Abbado. "Music forges a bond beyond all borders," was written on a piece of paper. "You'll probably never be able to listen this CD, but when reading the text, the melody will automatically sound in your ears. We share the same dream—that all men will be brothers one day."

Touched, I wiped away a few tears.

"One can count real friends on one hand," I thought to myself. I closed my eyes and thought back to our joint fight of the past thirty years. That struggle was almost ended by my umpteenth stroke.

"Let's not give up now," I encourage myself. "I will continue to fight peacefully, even though I'm paralyzed, to my last breath."

I turned to the Lieutenant Colonel. "Can I have my breviary?"

I reread the prophetic words of Isaiah:

> Comfort my people, says your God.
> Speak tenderly to Jerusalem, and proclaim to her
> That her hard service has been completed.

The package also contained a red hardcover book with "*Cong Dong Cung Hat*" written in gold letters. A hymnbook! Where did that come from? For years, the Vietnamese bishops had asked in vain to be allowed to publish a hymnbook.

"I dedicate this inspiring book to you," Van Loi had written on the first page. "Friends from the United States gave it to me. Be careful, because the ink isn't dry yet. I hope it will bring you much joy. Isn't singing like praying twice?"

My mouth dropped open when I saw the *Song of Peace* by Kim Long on the first page. I hummed the melody while browsing the book; the whole liturgical cycle was covered in it. As happy as a child I pressed the book against my heart. I haven't often received gifts in my life, but the ones I got were all very dear to me. I was reminded of the toy car I got from my brother Nguyen San when I was a child.

Ngoc was absorbed in a tabloid. My stomach turned at the sight of the garish photos and headlines on the cover.

"News from the front?" I asked teasingly. "Which Famous Vietnamese hopped into bed with another man or woman this week? Who is divorced or married for the umpteenth time? And what does the headline 'He did it with my best friend' mean? What has this guy been up to?"

My comments didn't amuse Ngoc. "It relaxes me to read this."

"I'm surprised that details about the sex lives of Vietnamese people can relax you."

"Are you lecturing me?" she said indignantly. "I read what I want. This is, indeed, no reading for priests. Because sex is taboo for you guys.

"But are you sure that no priest would buy this tabloid?" Kien intervened in the debate. "In how many countries is your Church ravaged by pedophilia scandals?"

What could I say to that? As if it was my fault that some of my colleagues are abusing their position of power to rape children.

"Pedophilia is a shameful crime, and when priests are guilty, they deserve double punishment because of their duty to set an example. But don't worry, I've never bought your rag, and I would put my hand in the fire first, and this also applies to all priests I know."

"What bothers you in this tabloid?" Kien interjected.

"The total lack of morality. For purely commercial reasons, one shamelessly exploits the most intimate feelings of humankind. Are we going to educate our children in such a climate? Of course, the Communists can't be bothered because they don't attach any importance to family values."

"Stop moralizing, preacher!" Ngoc exclaimed angry. "Do you really think I'm going to leave my husband and children because I read this magazine?" She made a dismissive gesture. "Don't exaggerate!"

A sign along the road said that there were still 165 kilometers to Vinh and 490 to Hanoi. We were driving inland through the jungle. The exits mentioned places that I'd never heard of.

"Are those the New Economic Zones?" I asked Kien.

He nodded.

How many millions of South Vietnamese were deported to these remote areas after 1975? I once wrote a little manual for the deported Catholics. From my childhood, I knew how hard it was to turn a piece of jungle into fertile farmland. Moreover, the people had to cede 40 percent of the harvest to the authorities and 30 percent to the area managers.

I remember the stories of some people who fled these areas. They could barely survive there and discipline was similar to that in the re-education camps.

"I wonder what has happened to the millions of South Vietnamese who have been deported to this region," I confronted Kien. "And what has happened to the children who were born over here."

He didn't react immediately.

"Do you know more?" I further challenged Kien.

But he remained silent.

"It is indeed difficult to talk about one of the great ignominies of the communist regime. How many have died over here or languished in those dungeons of society?"

Kien became more brave. "Once again you are exaggerating. Millions of people?" He laughed. "You don't know what that means."

I wanted to react, but the Lieutenant Colonel spoke first. "You are partly right. Not all New Economic Zones were successful. But don't worry. In many places, they still exist."

We now approached the first mountains of the central highlands. That is the home of the indigenous people of Vietnam. The French called those destitute hill tribes the *Montagnards*. I am thinking about the Bahnar, the Jarai, and the Bru. These tribes are the oldest original inhabitants of Southeast Asia. Today they remain faithful to their customs, religion, language, culture, and traditional costumes. But more than 80 percent live below the poverty line. They slowly but surely become extinct.

We drove past a military area where all access roads were barricaded by the army.

"Do you know why no one is allowed to enter this area?"

"How would I know?" said Ngoc. "Because of the danger of the army's shooting exercises?"

"No. Because there are concentration camps. And the government doesn't want any prying eyes. As the cornerstone of the regime, the army contributes to the oppression of anyone who stands up for more freedom and change."

Kien tried to challenge me. "Feel free to talk to the nurse about your political activities," he smiled.

"I don't have anything to hide. Yes, on the eve of the Tenth Congress of the Communist Party in 2006, I signed the *Democratic Manifesto* of the Bloc 8406 movement. And later, I stood at the cradle of the Vietnamese Progress Party, the VNPP. I'm not at all ashamed about that; quite the contrary."

"That manifesto and this new party were a provocation!"

"Since when is peacefully defending freedom provocative? Do you remember the main topic of discussion at the five-yearly Congress of the Communist Party that took place a few weeks after the founding of Bloc 8406? The scandal involving corrupt politicians and party officials who had used millions of dollars of development aid to buy luxury cars and bet on football matches in England and Spain."

"Corruption is indeed a bottleneck, but the government takes firm action against it," emphasized Kien. "At that time, the Minister of Transport, who was a compulsive gambler, was arrested."

"Indeed, but he was released at the end of the congress."

"Why?" asked Ngoc amazed.

I didn't give Kien time to react. "Because in our country the politicians decide who will be prosecuted by the court. And any investigation into a senior person's activities is automatically stopped when his network is set in motion. Do you know that the journalist who reported on the betting scandal in the newspapers was sentenced to two years in prison while the minister who is addicted to gambling walked free? Even worse, the next day he took his old job again. Who knows, maybe that man is gambling with money from the government again."

"What would you know about that? When you accuse people you must provide proof. And in this case, you are completely mistaken. The man has been given a different job. He is no longer allowed to handle money."

"I can't remember the fine points exactly, but you must have heard that he was promoted to a higher position with the mere objective of getting rid of him. Now he earns even more than before. Do you, sister, now understand what kind of country we live in?" I turned to Kien. "I respect you as a person, but how can you continue to defend this corrupt system?"

Ngoc looked bewildered, but I continued. "For years, the communist regime tried to prevent all contacts of members of the Vietnamese opposition with foreign journalists. That happened also during the visit of U.S. President Bush to Hanoi in late 2006. Streets were sealed off, phone connections cut off, and my email blocked."

"I still remember the picture of the U.S. President under a bust of Ho Chi Minh," said Ngoc.

"You've got a good memory!"

She blushed.

"What is still needed is the cultivation of critical sense. You are an intelligent woman, sister. But you should learn to analyze the propaganda that the regime dishes up every day. What a farce that image of President Bush at the bust of Ho Chi Minh was! Just imagine! Thanks to her archenemy, the United States, Vietnam became a member of the World Trade Organization. Both the communist regime and Bush only counted the money and the interests of the multinationals and the banks. Like Pontius Pilate, Bush washed his hands of responsibility while I was once again the first to disappear behind bars. And then the Lieutenant Colonel alleges that I am a puppet of the Americans! Only if you take a critical look at the world, sister, you will see through the propaganda."

But Kien also wanted to convince Nurse Ngoc that he was right. "Don't be misled! The real reason for the Reverend's arrest was his attempt to topple the regime!"

"How then?"

"Paper is testimony. Just a moment." He looks in his file again. "Somewhere here I have something called the text of the Lac Hong Coalition that you cosigned."

"Don't bother. One phrase sums up everything: 'through free elections allowing Vietnam to develop and flourish in a societal system based on virtue, democracy, freedom, and respect for the law.'"

I turned to Nurse Ngoc. "You heard well: free elections with several parties and not only the communist party as is the case today. But also the participation of a broad range of democratic parties that defend the real needs of the population and that want to put an end to the Chinese dominance that increases each day. Who would you vote for? The communists? Or would you vote for the Vietnamese Populist Party, the VPP; the Action Party of the Vietnamese People, the PAP; the Vietnamese Reform Party, the VRP; the Democratic Party Vietnam, the DVP; or our Vietnamese Progress Party, the VNPP?"

The sister was startled. I felt I had touched her conscience, but above all that, I suppose she was thinking about the privileges of her children.

"I won't force you to choose," I smiled. "Free elections are unfortunately not going to happen in the near future, because all the leaders of these new political parties have been, in recent years, imprisoned in concentration camps. In this country, anyone who raises his or her voice is silenced. In my case, this literally happened."

"Oh, that was you!" Ngoc reacted with surprise. "I remember the TV news of that time."

She turned to Kien. "Why was the Reverend treated like this?"

"You just heard it yourself—because of his political actions and his attempt to topple the regime."

"Why was he gagged?"

"The Reverend further acted violently by slandering our country in the presence of international observers."

"What did he say?"

I intervened immediately. "I shouted, 'Down with Communism!' and 'The Communists apply the law of the jungle.' Didn't I have the right to shout these words at the end of a showcase trial? When you appear in court for the fourth time, you have learned that this country's justice system does not aspire for justice but oppression. Such a regime should disappear."

Traffic slowed down as the road increasingly narrowed. There was a police checkpoint, but our ambulance was waved through. Colleagues of the government services always wave at one another. However, the woman whose papers were checked was less fortunate. She even had to open the trunk of her car. She apparently refused to pay a bribe, because the officers were now looking for violations of the law so that they could give her a fine. These days, only those who pay are not bothered.

A little further on we were approaching the Kim Lien exit. A sign in English and Vietnamese invites passersby to visit the birthplace of Ho Chi Minh. "As the region has few cultural or natural sights or landmarks, they have fabricated one for the benefit of the local tourism industry," I observed knowingly.

Despite my intention to deal a little less harshly with the Lieutenant Colonel, I couldn't help but ask: "Did you already go on a pilgrimage to that place?" I grinned. "I'm sure you know all the songs that praise Ho Chi Minh by heart, right? Is that still compulsory teaching material in order to make progress in your career in the Party ranks?"

He remained silent at first since he knew that I despise the historic communist leader. But a moment later he reacted. "I barely see any difference with the songs that glorify Our Lady of La Vang. You know those songs by heart."

I heard Phuc's sardonic laugh and the approving noises the driver made.

"You'd love to declare Ho Chi Minh a saint. But he can't even come close to the Mother of God who really was a holy woman. The whole artificially created cult around Ho Chi Minh is fake. And you know that only too well. The house where he was born is not the original, but it was specially built."

I waited a few moments, but got no response.

"It is said that there is even a family altar, an altar where his ancestors are honored. Isn't that strange for a Communist and an atheist?"

Still nothing. But I didn't give up.

"Do you remember my article that I gave you six months ago about the mythologizing of the figure of Ho Chi Minh? Do you agree that this ordinary opportunist is at the root of all the problems our country faces?"

Kien remained silent.

"Or have you been banned from reading that article by your superiors?"

His face turned as red as a tomato.

"That so-called ascetic who was primarily a womanizer. That nationalist who only used Communism to free Vietnam from foreign invaders. The man who . . ."

"Stop mocking the father of the nation immediately!" shouted Phuc.

"It's incredible how the fable of 'holy' Ho Chi Minh is still imprinted on minds," I said unperturbed.

Phuc turned around and pointed his gun at me.

Only now Kien intervened.

"Everybody shut up!"

"But . . ."

"I don't want to hear another word about Ho Chi Minh."

We approached Vinh, the capital of Nghe An province. This port city is located on the banks of the Blue River and has a population of a quarter of a million people. The mountain at the city entrance is mostly covered in pine trees. The forest still hasn't recovered from the bombing during the war. Never before had I seen such a drab environment. Striking in that endless row of concrete cubicles are dark brown apartment blocks, a donation of "comrades" from former East Germany. These apartments with their large windows are completely unsuited to the climatic conditions in Vietnam.

"Is there always so much wind?" I asked Nurse Ngoc.

She smiled. "We are used to that. Typhoons regularly sweep through the city. Therefore, a folk saying goes that the typhoon was born in Vinh. Flooding also regularly occurs since the sea is indeed close by."

Trucks moved bumper to bumper, accelerated and slowed down after a few meters, then braked again, emitting tons of CO_2. The whole city stinks of pollution. Half an hour later, we had barely moved a kilometer.

"I know the way," said Ngoc. "Unfortunately, the Main Road runs through the city centre. You best take the next road left, the Dao Tang, towards the museum. And then go right. This parallel route avoids the traffic around the bus station."

We were not alone in choosing this detour around the Museum of the Nghe Tinh.

"Is that museum named after two provinces?"

"You're much smarter than I thought," Kien joked. He obviously was in a better mood now. This was obviously a showcase of which the regime continued to be proud. In front of us, schoolchildren in their red uniforms boarded a bus.

"On May 1, 1930, farmers in the provinces of Nghe An and Ha Tinh, the two poorest in the country, revolted against the French. They established local soviets that took over the government, and they created village militias. A column of thousands of farmers who marched to the provincial capital of Vinh was bombed, and the rebellion was brutally suppressed by the foreign legion in 1931," Kien proudly said.

The loudspeakers bellowed out communist militant songs in an effort to keep the "sacred fire" of the revolution burning within the population. What a contrast with the resignation of the hundreds of Party officials and civil servants that are sauntering about in their suits around noon.

"Are we going to eat?" Ngoc asked. "I'm hungry."

Kien opened the wicker basket with provisions. He was startled. "One drink, two sandwiches per person and a small dessert. For five people! And this is supposed to be our food for the whole day?"

"It's all they have given me. I phoned the hospital kitchen yesterday."

"Is that man deaf? Or doesn't he know how to write?"

"We'll share whatever we have," I said. "We won't really starve from hunger."

"What about all that traffic? Who knows at what time we'll arrive this evening in the camp Nam Ha?"

Kien turned to Ngoc. "Do you know a restaurant in this neighborhood that gives fast service?"

"Further down, near the station you'll find one after another. But they're probably full at this hour."

"Stop!" Kien ordered the driver. "Park in the second row and stay in the car. Phuc and I will get the food quickly." He ordered Ngoc and me to wait on the sidewalk.

In the crowded restaurant Kien and Phuc showed their identification. The waitress called the big boss. Meanwhile, I had a chat with a woman in traditional costume. I recognized the striped dress with the dominant red color. She belonged to the tribe of the Bahnar.

"Made by my own hands!" she said promoting her products.

"Why do you live in Vinh?"

"Coffee. The establishment of coffee plantations on our ancestral lands. Twenty years ago, we were forced to leave the central highlands. The move to the city was a nightmare. We had no choice. My husband is partially disabled, and I suffer with back pain. I can't possibly work on a plantation. Over here I hope to give a better future to our children. Thank God my son and daughter are good students. I have to feed four with the sales of these homemade craftworks."

Ngoc looked interested.

"That's far better quality than the industrial fabric that you see everywhere. Also better than in the so-called 'traditional villages' visited by Western tourists," the woman said, giving a big smile. "I'll give you a special price."

"Those two napkins?"

"200,000 dong."

"That's expensive."

"Normally you will pay 200,000 for one of these. Here I offer you two for the price of one. Look at the quality," she tried to convince Ngoc.

"100,000."

"I can't sell these for less than 150,000."

"130,000. And not a dong more."

I looked on, amused. Bargaining is not my thing. The women made a deal. They were both happy.

"Do you dream of returning to your homeland?"

"Of course. Maybe in a few years when my children graduate." But she hesitated. "But, hey, how can we make a living over there?" I heard resignation in her voice. "I'm afraid that . . . I will have to stay here. The highlands are still isolated from the rest of the world. During the demonstrations ten years ago, many hundreds of my tribe were arrested, including some family members. I haven't heard from them since. What happened to them? Are they still alive?"

The woman sighed. "It's so hard to live here in Vinh according to our old traditions and values. However, I will live and die as a member of the Bahnar."

"I appreciate the determination with which you keep the tradition alive," said I. "Keep your spirits up and persevere in what you do."

However, I fear that her culture will only be appreciated for its true value when her generation is gone, but I didn't tell her that.

The woman was delighted, but she was a realist. "It hurts a lot that it can be so difficult to pass on that tradition and our values to my children. The influence of their circle of friends is great. Not to be bullied my son wears a baseball cap and a T-shirt with the logo of an American university. He is afraid to show who he really is."

She suddenly noticed the cross on my collar. "Are you a Catholic priest?"

I nodded. "But en route to a concentration camp."

The woman made a little bow out of respect and pulled a book from under her apron. "This will surely interest you."

The Struggle Continues. I stood transfixed. It was picture book about the Catholic mass demonstration from two years ago.

"Preceded by the bishop, we were hundreds of thousands of believers who walked peacefully in the streets," she said. "At the end of the demonstration, the police charged. A priest was seriously injured in the confrontation. Another priest who visited him in the hospital was thrown from the first floor of the building. He is still in a coma."

"I was here when that happened. I was visiting my brother," Ngoc said. "I had never seen a demonstration of praying people. I also remember the sirens blaring. We were so scared that evening we were afraid to leave my brother's apartment."

"This book was printed illegally," the woman whispered. "The CD at the back contains a short amateur film that records the brutal behavior of the police. 100,000 dong."

I sighed. "Only five U.S. dollars. If I could, I would even give you ten dollars, but I don't even have one dong. But I have an idea. I have a book of Vietnamese hymns, which was published in the United States. You could sell it or use it in your parish. Can't we swap?"

The woman leafed through the book and immediately agreed. She even gave me a small, hand-woven cross for free.

"Come and eat!" shouted Phuc. I stuffed the book and the cross in the bag and took leave from the woman with a small bow. I looked Ngoc straight in the eye. I was sure that she wouldn't betray me.

In the restaurant, the waiters ran to and fro. In the background, I could faintly hear Communist fight songs, but they were drowned out by the hustle and bustle. Some bottles of water were placed on the table, and we were immediately served eel soup, followed by a plate of *banh beo*, a typical dish of Hue. I enjoyed the pieces of shrimp and pork on rice flour dough with herbs.

A little over ten minutes later, Kien ordered us to leave the restaurant.

"What about coffee and dessert?" I teasingly asked. "I'm sure that Nurse Ngoc would like that."

Kien looked sour. "Be happy that we've given you some food."

When I got into the car, I looked at the Bahnar woman. Around her neck hung a ribbon with woven crosses. We understood each other without words. Faith is the most invisible, but also the strongest, language that exists on earth.

6

3:00 p.m.

The small airport located just outside Vinh was as miserable as the region that we were driving through. We were in the poorest province of Vietnam.

I peeked into the book while Kien dozed off after the delicious meal.

"Ascension was a milestone in the history of our diocese and the Church in Vietnam," the bishop writes in the preface. "Whoever thinks he can eradicate the faith is wrong because the religious dimension is embedded in the genes of every human being. You cannot destroy the soul of man. The more you suppress faith, the more it rises like a phoenix from the ashes." I'm impressed and must once again reconsider my opinion—apparently not all bishops are lackeys of the regime.

I got goose bumps when I turned the page. Spread over two pages, a photograph shows the first row of protestors. Dozens of priests around the bishop carry a banner with the slogan "Religious Freedom or Death." In 2000, I had hung that slogan on the church tower of Nguyet Bieu.

I continued to browse the book. What a sea of people. I was locked up in a camp at the time. It was only last year, during my stay at the archdiocese in Hue, that I read the reports on the *Asia*

News and the Catholic press agency *Ucanews* websites. Somewhere I read the figure of half a million participants. At the time, I could hardly believe it. But this book clearly shows that the demonstration was unprecedented in the history of Vietnam.

The texts on the banners sound familiar to me: "Justice Now," "Hands off our church in Dong Hoi," "Give all church property back," and "We need real freedom of religion." People applauded a delegation of Buddhists led by monks in their orange robes. Surrounded by their holy flags, they carried the banner "All religions = same struggle."

I immediately thought of the prophetic words of Monsignor Van Thuan and the music of the apotheosis of Beethoven's *Ninth Symphony* sounded in my ears. Van Thuan was right—the Buddhists are our brothers.

This enthusiasm made me once again realize that that my lifelong peaceful struggle for freedom has not been in vain. All my actions, letters, calls, and manifestos helped to keep the pilot light burning. By sowing mustard seeds for almost four decades under difficult conditions, the unthinkable was now becoming reality. The almost exterminated Church in North Vietnam suddenly seemed alive and well. My thoughts go to the Thai Ha parish in Hanoi. Phan Van Loi will go there tonight peacefully demonstrating for the restitution of the confiscated Redemptorist monastery.

Overcome by a sense of bliss, I fell asleep.

"What's this?" Kien shook me awake. "Where does this book come from?"

Still drunk with sleep, I didn't know what was happening to me.

"This is illegal literature," fulminated Kien. "I am obliged to draw up a report about this."

Painfully, I tried to sit up straight.

"Who gave you this book, when and where? Last name, first name, and physical description."

"I don't know what you're talking about."

"The possession of illegal publications carries heavy penalties."

I didn't say a word.

"No? Then I will have to interrogate the nurse."

Ngoc was petrified.

"She's got nothing to do with it."

"That's for me to decide."

"Ngoc, where does that book come from?"

She blushed, but she didn't say a word.

"Obstructing an investigation is punishable. And anyone in this country who has a criminal record . . ."

"Leave the nurse out of this," I intervened immediately. "She's got nothing to do with it."

"Ah! So you are the culprit! Who has given you this? Last name, first name, and physical description."

"I got it from a passerby when I was waiting on the sidewalk outside the restaurant."

He was seething with anger. "That's unbelievable," he shouted. "Two minutes. I leave you alone two minutes, and you pull a trick on me! Who has given this to you? And where is your other book?"

"I traded it for this one."

"With whom?"

"Someone I don't know. We barely spoke to one another."

"Did you see anything?" Kien asked Phuc.

He looked surprised. "What do you mean? I was with you in the restaurant!"

"And you, driver?"

He also denied in all tonalities. "Watching traffic. Searching for parking."

"Is this a conspiracy?" exclaimed Kien.

Suddenly his eye falls on the woven cross that was lying on my knee.

"Ah! That red color." He beamed. "That will please the secret service of Vinh. You can't trust these mountain people."

"Ngoc, can you confirm that the woman in traditional costume in front of the restaurant is the culprit?"

"She didn't hear that conversation."

"I'm asking the nurse, not you!"

"I . . . didn't . . . see anything. I was . . . looking around to see if I knew anybody."

"Why do you protect her?"

"I protect nobody."

"You can be sure there will be a sequel to this story. This book is confiscated." The man opened his travel bag and took some notes.

"I insist that you include in the report that this has happened as a result of the visit to a restaurant during a prison transport. Such a visit is not allowed, right? Only sanitary stops are permitted."

Kien gritted his teeth and put his papers back in his bag.

"The Typhoon over Vinh died down," I said almost whispering.

Ngoc, who was once again engrossed in her gossip magazine, bit her tongue to keep from laughing.

A sign indicated that there were still 65 kilometers to go to Thanh Hoa. I opened my eyes widely. I only have bad memories of that region.

It was mid-December 1983, when I was taken from the courthouse in the city to the notorious camp of Thanh Cam in the jungle. Ho Chi Minh's statement "*Khong Gi Quy Hon Duc Lap Tu Do*"—"Nothing is more precious than independence and freedom"—marked the entrance to the camp. Communism and cynicism go hand in hand. But that was the most cynical joke that I, as a life-long fighter for freedom and independence, have ever seen.

I arrived in a barrack with about a hundred prisoners.

"Hello. Nguyen Van Ly. I'm a priest. I just got a promotion," he smiled to his neighbor.

The man hardly reacted.

I asked my other neighbor, "How long have you been here?"

But he didn't react either.

"Doctor Huang from Saigon," said the man in front of me stoically. "I came here eight and a half years ago."

"Immediately after the communist takeover?" I answered in surprise.

The man nodded.

"What happened?"

"Nothing," said Huang without any emotion.

"What do you mean?"

"Really nothing. I was summoned to attend a 'Thirty-Day Class.' But since then I haven't even been interrogated. And I never got an answer to all my questions.

"Are there more people in your situation?"

"You'll find in this barrack dozens of executives of the former South Vietnamese regime: lawyers, teachers, journalists, writers, professors, entrepreneurs . . . whatever you want."

"How are the living conditions?"

"Very harsh . . . Discipline is extremely severe . . . Strict rules for waking up and meals . . . Follow my advise. Go to sleep now. Tomorrow morning we'll have to wake at six a.m. The work in the felling industry is physical and heavy."

"Faster," the guard shouted during my first "working day." "This row of trees has to be dragged away and stacked today."

"How can this be done?" I objected.

He grabbed my collar. "What are you thinking, greenhorn? Are you going to tell us what has to be done over here? Forward—from now on you'll be the first in line."

"Stop protesting," my neighbor whispered fiercely. "If you make him angry he'll use his whip." He glanced over his shoulder. "Usually all of us work slowly. He can't whip everyone. And pretend that you're gritting your teeth all the time."

During the midday break, I flopped down. "Is it like this every day? Such monotonous and exhausting work! And dangerous too. What would happen if someone stumbles and that tree falls on his leg?"

"Bad luck for him."

"Bad luck?"

"Hey, what do you think? They will ask you for advice?"

My fellow prisoners burst out laughing.

"Sensibility and idealists have no place here. Over here only production quotas are important. Each month hundreds of trees must be processed. And if we don't meet the pre-established production quotas, we'll get less food."

"Even less food? I . . ."

When the screaming guard appeared we all grew silent. He indeed took out his whip.

"Left your post?" he shouted to an older prisoner.

"I urgently had to go to the toilet."

"Do you still not know the work schedule?"

"It was urgent," the man defended himself. "I suffer from diarrhea."

"Do you know what is urgent?" the guard shouted. "Over there an American bomb has to be cleared."

The man looked perplexed.

"Right away and use both your hands."

In the evening, after nine hours of hard labor, we trudged back to the camp under the supervision of armed guards, their rifles at the ready. "Silence and march in formation," the guard shouted.

"Now it's time for the re-education session," my neighbor whispered.

"Really?"

"Three hours."

"What?"

"We'll sing *Ten Thousand Years*," the teacher said after everyone was seated.

I could barely keep my eyes open. "What nonsense!" I thought. "Wishing the long-dead Ho Chi Minh a long life is indeed nonsensical."

"Hands in the air," we were ordered when singing the refrain.

"You're new here?" said the woman, standing in front of me. "Can't you sing?" She pressed a songbook into my hand.

"Sorry, but I can't read," I said dismissively. "Not anymore . . ." I added cynically.

"Fortunately you've got two hands."

"Why?"

"To work of course. Because working is very important in the Marxist doctrine. And especially important in the framework of re-education." She adjusted her glasses. "Does anyone know why?"

No reaction. "We have treated this subject last week!" the teacher said angrily. "Work not only gives meaning to our life, it also prevents the crimes that you have committed."

I almost keel over hearing so much nonsense.

"After a lesson on the history of the Vietnamese revolution and an overview of the crimes of the Americans and the South Vietnamese, tomorrow we will talk about the achievements of our government," the woman imperturbably continued to speak. "Today, in groups, we'll discuss a number of articles that were published in our Party Newspaper *Nhan Dan* and the army newspaper *Quan Doi Nhan Dan*."

She handed out copies of the newspaper. "As always per table in groups of four persons. First, read the text attentively and then comment on the issues from the perspective of the Marxist doctrine."

Our group was given a text about the visit of a Chinese trade mission to Hanoi.

"Look at our new colonizers!" I said in a loud voice.

The teacher didn't know what was happening to her. "I thought that you couldn't read?"

"You can see from afar that these are Chinese people!" I replied.

Everyone burst out laughing.

"Chinese people wearing custom-made suits not army uniforms. That is strange," I continue. There was even more general amusement now. "They have however only one objective:

plundering Vietnam of all its resources as they have done for centuries." Everyone went wild.

The woman left the room in tears. Some prisoners jumped on their table and shrieked with laughter. But the mood changed when the camp director and armed guards burst into the room.

"Mr. Ly," he said in a measured tone. He perused the thick file that he carried. "A priest who pretends to be illiterate, but who spurs people on and who provokes one of our best teachers. That does not sound very Catholic. The usual punishment would be three months solitary confinement. But on your first day here I would like to do you a favor as a welcoming present."

He smiled. "From now on you will attend the lessons in silence." He raised his voice: "If in the future you utter even one word, I don't know whether you'll ever leave the isolation cell." Without another word he turned around and left the room.

Every day I stared at the lamps on the ceiling for hours on end. Each time I was tempted to denounce all the nonsense that was spoken, I hummed in my mind the *Song of Peace* composed by Kim Long. And in order not to suffer psychologically during these everlasting, very boring sessions, I retreated in my cocoon and I concentrated on prayer.

"Will you help me, as promised, to write a letter to my family?" begged a prisoner.

I looked dismayed. "Not now. I'm too tired. I must go directly to sleep. I'll do it next Sunday or during the *Tet* festival in two weeks when we're usually given three days off."

"Don't they turn out the lights during the night?" asked a new prisoner who was lying next to me.

"You have a lot to learn. That happens for "security reasons" . . . and I also heard that our Great Leader, Ho Chi Minh, the Man of the Eternal Light, was afraid of darkness."

"Hey you! Keep your hands above the bed covers and turn around," the guard shouted to the new prisoner. "You've got to sleep with your face turned to the door. I will only say this once," he warned.

I shook my head. This guard, who scrupulously follows the orders, was an alcoholic like many others.

"For your own wellbeing, don't ask questions," I whispered to the new prisoner. "Most guards are driven by hatred, hunger for power, and sadism."

"Why?"

"That's how they vent their frustrations and compensate for their inferiority complex, because this isn't a prestigious job in the eyes of society. Be aware that nobody hates you. Otherwise this can lead to a humiliating treatment and confiscating the goods that your family members will send to you."

During a beating in the barrack two weeks later, the guards didn't intervene.

"What's happening here?" asked the new prisoner, surprised.

"Beatings are, as you know, a daily occurrence. But the guards also respect the balance of power between the clans because they contribute to peace and stability. And you're not blind to see that some of them, who continuously enter and leave the barracks, try to get a piece of the pie on each occasion."

"There's something I don't understand."

I looked up. "What?"

"You fight always against the arbitrariness in the camp. Why don't you handle this now?"

"I should do that from nature. But now I'm thinking about the words of St. Paul in the *Letter to the Romans*: 'Bless them that persecute you, bless and do not curse.' The guards don't have an easy life either. They reside with their families in a separate section, and they live isolated from the world."

One month later I was really upset. "Why is this elderly prisoner is given the toughest task, while the lighter work once goes to this young man?"

"Don't talk that way!" the director sternly reacted. "He's rewarded because he's making great progress on the path of re-education. I wish you would also."

"Don't let me laugh! He's just a loyal informant who reports every day on what happens in the barracks."

"You'll end up in solitary for the umpteenth time with the strictest regime! Guards, take him away!"

"Here we go again, halved portions. And during the next couple of months, the eternal silence will be only broken by the rattling of the keys of the guards who bring the food."

"How do you like your stay in the isolation cell?" The director smiled another month later.

I looked dismayed.

"I've heard you've had an incident."

I looked at the guard. "Thanks for sending your boss."

"What's the problem?" smiled the director.

"I'm suffering from diarrhea. And I had no choice other than to catch my stools in my bowl."

The director and the guard were laughing loudly.

"That's the joke of the year! But why in your bowl?"

"Can't you understand? To prevent the diarrhea from landing on the floor on which I've to sleep."

"That's not my problem. Guard, will you rinse that with water first?

"What do you think?" the man furiously reacted. "Am I a cleaning lady?"

The director continued to giggle. "Guard, this is an order."

He took the bowl and reluctantly went to the toilet to clean it.

"I don't have a brush. Here's your bowl," he reacted after his return when he got the meal in it.

"This still stinks of stools," I reacted bitterly. "Am I supposed to eat this?"

"That's up to you," replied the director.

"The prison library is open," I invited Doctor Huang on a Sunday morning. "You're coming with me?"

"No thanks. I'm surprised you're interested in the books and magazines that are totally pervaded with the ideal of 'socialist realism.' You'll see life-sized posters on the wall that exude optimism and heroism. They want to spur everyone into more enthusiasm for the realization of the communist ideal. I wish you success!"

"I don't know what happened," I replied. "Since I saw the librarian yesterday, I feel the need to challenge that sullen man who is the antipode of that fake ideal. I'll pretend interest in Marxist-Leninist ideology.

"In that case I'm interested in going with you," he smiled.

"Am I allowed to ask a question?" I asked the librarian in a polite way.

"Go ahead," reacted the man enthusiast. "You're the first to do so since I've arrived here."

"During my study of Marxism-Leninism . . . I am wondering . . . when the final phase of socialism, namely communism, is built . . . will there still be thefts and pilfering?"

The librarian was petrified and didn't answer immediately.

"No," I smiled, "because everything will be already pilfered during socialism."

Doctor Huang bite on his tongue to keep from laughing, but the man became angry. I calmed him down.

"I'm sorry . . . That was only a joke," I still was teasing him, but became more serious. "But I have another, a serious question. I guess you'll know the answer!"

"What then," the librarian responded curiously.

"What will be the result of the elections?"

"We'll know that on Sunday evening," the man smiled. "But this will for sure be a great victory for the Communist Party."

But I shook my head. "Nobody will ever know."

"Why not?" the librarian reacted with surprised.

"Yesterday, someone stole the election results from the office of the Central Committee of the party."

"Get out, you! And never come back!" shouted the librarian.

3:00 p.m.

He kicked Doctor Huang and me out of the library.

"Why are you so nervous?" I stated with my friend, Doctor Huang.

"I hope that one of my family members will come to visit me today."

"Are you afraid that nobody will come?"

Doctor Huang started weeping.

"And your wife?" I asked.

Doctor Huang was silent but then stammered, "I saw her . . . for the last time . . . two years ago. She doesn't even . . . answer my letters. I guess she has another man . . . And I've also lost contact with my daughter. But I keep on writing every month . . . You're expecting someone?"

"I hope my sister Tri Hieu will find this *anus mundi*," I reacted. "And maybe one of my parents. But they're already in their eighties. We shall see."

"Where are they coming from?"

"Near Saigon."

"You can't make that trip in one day. Due to the poor condition of the roads, driving the sixty miles from Thanh Hoa takes almost ten hours on the bus. And there are several miles remaining from the bus stop to the camp."

"Hoa, Trong, Duc, and Van Ly, visit," shouted the guard at the entrance of the barrack.

I stood and looked back to Doctor Huang who started weeping again.

"My help and support. Once again!" I welcomed my sister warmly.

She started weeping. "I constantly asked to visit, but I was not allowed to come earlier. I became desperate; it's almost been a year since we've seen each other."

Tri Hieu looked at me attentively and continued: "Don't worry. Every time it is permitted, I'll be there, even if you should be transferred to a camp in the north."

I became emotional. "Your mere presence makes me incredibly happy. Do you know what touches me most?"

Tri shook her head.

"Your warm voice. That always reminds me of Mom. Your look says more than a thousand words, and your tender hands on mine recharge my batteries."

I made a circling motion with my forefinger. Tri understood immediately what I meant—every conversation is recorded.

"My return to the barracks in a while will be painful," I whispered.

"Why?"

"Most of the prisoners never get visitors, letters, food packages, or medicine."

"So you'll share what I've brought for you."

"That'll be absolutely necessary. Most prisoners can't survive without solidarity. I'm glad you've brought a blanket with you. My friend, Doctor Huang, will be very pleased. And the medicine will also be very useful; we can prevent people dying of malaria or dysentery."

"How's the atmosphere in the barracks?" Tri asked after a short silence.

I sighed. "Yesterday a man threw himself on the high-voltage electric fence. He was completely desperate. Coexistence is difficult because of the lack of privacy, the diversity of the prison population, the incessant noise, and the ever disturbing broadcasts through loudspeakers. All this affects everybody's mind. The mood swings are difficult to bear.

"Why are you smiling?" My sister looked surprised.

"I'm thinking of an incident last week. After a hard morning of forced labor, I was looking forward to an afternoon nap. However, I couldn't rest because a small group continued to make noise. Nobody dared to go against that clique of former gangsters and thugs, but I went over to them and said, 'You have the right to eat and talk. However, all I ask is that you make less noise so that the other prisoners can rest a bit before going back to work.'"

"You were absolutely right! And then?"

"I returned to my place under a barrage of insults and obscenities. When we returned after the re-education session, the gang leader took revenge. His target was my water bucket that I got from you. Many wanted to have it. The man threw it on the ground, broke it, and cursed. But I remained calm and said, 'I'm sorry that something has upset you, and I regret that I don't have more things that you can destroy to make your anger subside. But there's one thing you should know.' 'What?' the man shouted. 'While you were taking revenge, I prayed for you, your wife, your children, and your parents. I hope that you'll be released quickly and that you can rejoin your loved ones.' Then I went to sleep."

"What happened next?

"The next morning, the gang leader sent one of his henchmen to ask me to go and see him. Some inmates feared for my safety, but I went straight to the gang leader. When I saw him, he immediately stood up and offered, to everyone's surprise, his apologies. 'I'm sorry for these recent events. That will not happen again.' Everyone looked surprised. 'I promise more respect . . . and I want to . . . become a Christian. Can I ask you to teach me?' I also had a bit of a fright. 'When your wish is sincere, I'll do that,' I answered. Immediately the news spread in the camp that I had not only been able to subdue a gang leader, but also that the man had begged him to become my student.

Tri was relieved. "That was a happy end! I'm glad you can help your fellow prisoners with their moral dispositions of mind also."

"Absolutely. At their request, I constantly guide prisoners and give explanations on Christianity and the interpretation of texts in the Bible. And every day I guide prisoners. A number have become Christians, but when the poet Nguyen Chi Thien asked for it, I felt that the time was not yet right. Three months ago, when I was caught secretly celebrating the Eucharist, I ended up in solitary confinement for a long time with heavy cuffs around my ankles.

"Oh my God! What did you do after your return to the barracks?"

"What do you think? Continue my work, but more hidden. When I got yet another warning from a guard to stop my pastoral activities, I replied, 'If you won the lottery, would not your heart overflow with joy? Would you not share that joy with your loved ones? Through my faith, I feel so much joy within me that I want to share it with my fellow prisoners. Why would I not be allowed to so?' The guard was impressed. More and more guards now urge me to continue the pastoral activities discreetly because they don't want trouble with the camp leaders."

"So the atmosphere is ameliorating in the barracks."

"That happens only step by step. Small things are happening all the time. Yesterday, for instance, another cellmate took me into confidence. 'Shame on me,' confessed the man. 'What for?' I asked. 'I've . . . the past months . . . a few times . . . food . . . from your bedside table . . . stolen . . . I want to compensate for that . . .' I interrupted him right away. 'I appreciate what you're saying, but let's turn the page.' 'Are you not angry?" the man responded. 'We are all suffering from hunger. Finding out that my food has been stolen is not funny. But with a piece of bread less, I've also survived. In my eyes, the theft of food in this place is no offense.' The man looked surprised. 'We can make our stay in this hell a small piece of heaven when everyone respects each other's belongings and shows more solidarity. Can we try this from now on?' The man nodded earnestly. 'Aren't all of us in the same boat?' I concluded.

"You're doing such a great job!" my sister reacted emotionally. "But how's the food? Because you've become so skinny."

"Daily life is completely dominated by . . . the lack of food," I sighed. "Furthermore the quality is very poor, and the kitchen staff hardly respect the elementary rules of hygiene. They've served rotten rice or cassava, potatoes, corn, or *bo bo*—that's cat food! But since a few months ago, things are changing."

"What happened?"

"I and my friend, Doctor Huang, were assigned to distribute the food. We hand out the meals correctly, even when there's meat on the menu, which only happens occasionally. It comes from the camp pigs and cattle."

"So things are going better now . . ."

"Don't go too fast! Shortly after our assignment we were distributing the meat in identical portions when the head guard ordered me, 'Ly, give me a kilogram of meat.' 'I can't possibly give you the prisoners' meat,' I replied. Surprised, the head guard left, but he later sent in a henchman with the same order. Again, I refused to give him the meat; this wasn't my first conflict with the head guard. When Doctor Huang and I took stock of the kitchen inventory, we discovered that he regularly stole large amounts of food. No one had ever done anything about it since that cruel man is known for his brutal treatment of prisoners. He is nicknamed 'the spinning gold.' Anyone who falls into disapproval is so harshly punished that if he wants to live, he has to bribe the man with gold."

"You're giving me the shivers. What did you do?"

"I lodged a complaint with the camp administration. As expected, the prison director didn't take it seriously, and then the head guard taught me a lesson. 'Carry these loads of the prisoners' excrement to the vegetable garden,' he shouted. That's the most feared punishment because of the unbearable stench and because I was not allowed to stop walking during that trip of a few kilometers.'

My sister gasped for breath.

"Next, the head guard order me, 'Move these heavy stones.' 'What's the sense of this?' I asked. 'You do what I say!' he answered while taking out his whip. One month later, when inspectors visited the prison camp, the camp directors intimidated me into remaining silent. But I was the only prisoner who stood up and said, 'I want to tell you some facts on the condition that you will protect me from being killed.' After I had made my report, I spent a few days in the inspectors' residential block. The head guard was transferred to another prison. Before his departure, I told him: 'I bear no grudge. I love you and wish you all the best.' But the man was unable to take that humiliation. Because he could do nothing else, he spat in my face."

"Driver, the radio. Time for the news," Kien ordered.

After three drum beats and the sound of trumpets, a voice was heard saying, "This is Radio 1. The Voice of Vietnam. The news."

"Over the first nine months of this year, the number of foreign tourists has increased to 4.7 million. The Ministry of Tourism expects that by the end of this year, the milestone of six million will be reached.

"Abroad. In Russia, the situation remains tense after Sunday's elections. The opposition has once more protested against the alleged fraud by the United Russia Party of Prime Minister Vladimir Putin. Mikhaïl Gorbatchov, the last Communist leader of the Soviet Union, has also called for new elections. However, Putin accuses Hillary Clinton, the U.S. Secretary of State for Foreign Affairs, of causing the unrest and of financially supporting the opposition.

"The weather. Today . . ."

"The meddlesomeness of the Americans is boundless," Kien said. "They want to lecture everybody. Now also in Russia. And where on earth don't they interfere?"

"Be honest!" I said. "What's this about the Americans and the Russian elections? That's completely unfounded propaganda."

Once again, traffic almost came to a standstill in the suburbs of Thanh Hoa, the umpteenth polluted industrial city we pass. Fortunately, there is a bypass for through traffic. Even more than in Vinh, the environmental pollution is obvious. Factory chimneys are spewing jet-black clouds of smoke, and along the roads, garbage is sometimes piled up meters high.

"This is the new *Agent Orange*. It isn't orange anymore, but black."

I look Kien straight in the eye. "No comment? Your wife and daughter are victims of the foul stuff that the Americans dropped over here in large quantities. Today, in front of our eyes, the same thing is happening and nobody protests."

He was clearly annoyed by my remark. "Nobody is perfect," he hesitantly replied. "Environmental pollution is indeed a problem. But the government has promised to address this problem as a priority. The Minister for the Environment has set up a working group in parliament."

"Do you still believe those empty promises? I make a dismissive gesture. "If I would believe all the promises of the government in the past years, Vietnam would be a paradise on earth by now."

Kien remained unmoved.

"Yes, a paradise!"

I turned to the others. "You have seen with your own eyes how there is environmental pollution everywhere. While everyone knows only too well the pollution of the Vietnam War, our country is faced with a potential ecological disaster that could be worse than the previous one. And you are placated by vague promises of incompetent ministers. Do you know how the ministers are recruited? Not based on their knowledge and their skills; only Party membership and loyalty to the government are of paramount importance."

I turned to Nurse Ngoc. "Communism does not solve any societal problem, but it saddles future generations with an additional burden that is heavier than the havoc the Americans have wrought over here."

7

6:00 p.m.

The closer we got to the capital, Hanoi, the busier the activity, but the roads improve. I noticed a factory under construction. The yard was invaded by a myriad of Chinese workers wearing yellow hardhats. The trucks were also made in China. On a site like this, you won't find any Vietnamese workers.

"Did you notice that there aren't any Vietnamese working over here?" I asked. "This time the workers are the first wave of the new Chinese invasion of Vietnam. And this is only the beginning. The Chinese always come back. It has always been like that for the past two thousand years. Today, history repeats itself, but in a different guise."

Ngoc frowned and Kien stared straight ahead, unmoved.

"In international politics, the whole world always looks at Beijing first. And after all these years, the ancient Chinese superiority surfaces again. Don't have any delusions. Vietnam is inevitably becoming a province of the Chinese once again. And what does our government do? Kowtow to the communist leaders in Beijing. Laos and Cambodia are already a Chinese protectorate, and now it's our turn."

Kien intervened, "Phuc is right, you always exaggerate."

"Why is every journalist or blogger that reports on the bauxite exploitation by the Chinese Chalco Group in the central highlands arrested and sentenced to long prison terms?"

"You can't give free rein to critics who are saying wildly ignorant things," Kien replied. "They are only bent on harming the interests of Vietnam and inciting the population."

"What about General Vo Nguyen Giap and the other former top Communist leaders who have signed the petition against Chalco?" I put myself straight. "Yes, you hear well Phuc! General Giap, the military mastermind who was responsible for the guerrillas not only against the French but also against the Americans. This man is 95 years old. Should he likewise be sentenced to a long prison term?"

"Damn it! China is a friendly nation," cried out the driver, who supported Phuc in this debate.

"A friendly nation?" I immediately reacted. "That is strange. About thirty years ago, in February 1979, the Chinese army invaded Vietnam. The border town of Lang Son was completely destroyed in retaliation for the Vietnamese occupation of Cambodia. But after seventeen days of fierce fighting the Vietnamese drove the blundering Chinese army back across the border, with the support of the Soviet Union."

I saw Nurse Ngoc blushing.

"The nurse remembers that, doesn't she?"

Tears ran down her cheeks. "My youngest uncle was killed in the fighting." She sobbed. "Do you know that my grandfather has buried his four sons? He himself died a few years later of grief."

These unexpected words cut to the bone. It was eerily quiet in the ambulance again.

"I'm sorry I've unintentionally ripped open old wounds," I said apologetically. "That was not my intention."

I saw that those words also touched Phuc. I had never seen him looking so crestfallen. Kien, who appeared to know more, also looked at Phuc.

"Brother Phuc," I said. "I . . ."

"You're not my brother," he shouted. "You are an enemy of the people."

"No, that is not true," I said. "Although you're on the side of my persecutors, you too are my brother."

Phuc dropped his gun and burst into tears. Open-mouthed and shaking his head, the driver divided his attention between the traffic and the tearful eyes of Phuc.

"We lived in Lang Son . . . A missile fell on our house . . . Father, mother, and my brother died . . . I was four years old . . . and I was wounded when I was removed from under the rubble . . . I always wear my hat . . . to hide the scar on my head . . . I was well taken care of . . . As a war orphan, I stayed in Hanoi . . . The Party has done everything for me . . . Without them I wouldn't be . . . alive. Thanks to them I got an education . . . Thanks to them I got a job . . . I remain a communist . . . until I die!"

"I respect who you are and what you are doing," I said in a soft tone. "Everyone is free to make choices in life. You have made yours, and I have made mine. But you should know that I'm not your enemy. If you need help, advice, or just a chat, my door is always open for you."

The tears in the eyes of Phuc were drying up.

"Have you ever heard about Beethoven?" I asked him.

He frowned.

I showed him the CD that I got from Phan Van Loi. "Two hundred years ago this composer made music that can still teach us a lot. 'All men will be brothers,' the lyrics say. I am convinced that this dream will come true."

I turned to Kien. "I myself am not perfect, but the communist regime isn't perfect either. If their loyal followers would be more critical of the policies of the government, who knows, a change could be set in motion from within the system. Because what is happening today in the central highlands goes far beyond the irrevocable destruction of the environment; a hidden agenda lies behind the tacit agreement with the Chinese looting of our bauxite. This is a great opportunity for the government in Hanoi to settle accounts with the *Montagnards*, the original inhabitants of the highlands who already are by far the poorest people in Vietnam. Their income is declining further and the fish and the wildlife are disappearing because of deforestation and pollution of the drinking water. When will the communists finally respect these ethnic minorities and realize that we are the stewards, not the owners, of this earth? We must, in the interest of future generations, stop the destruction of nature now. We must stop the Chinese who think they are above everything and everyone!"

I looked at Kien. "Oh, that's a difficult issue."

"Is that all you can say? Your wife and daughter are victims of the filth that the Americans have dumped here. A similar plague is happening right now before our eyes, but nobody speaks up. Worse, anyone who dares to expose this shameful operation is severely punished. Why? Because nobody has the courage to raise their voice against the Chinese who know that nothing and nobody can touch them."

I clung to my bed and I gasped for breath, because I felt dizzy. "The 'new' Chinese colonization does not happen on the battlefield. . . . The Chinese can't afford this because of their international position. . . . But the red bank note, the Chinese Yuan, is quietly taking the place of the green-back, the U.S. dollar. . . . On the diplomatic front, China claims the rich fishing grounds and huge reserves of oil and gas in the South China Sea, which have always been part of Vietnamese territory. . . . Shamelessly, they want to invade the Spratly archipelago, which has also always been a Vietnamese territory."

"These Chinese claims are unjustified," Kien agreed, "but our government doesn't give in so easily. As a warning, the army has even recently held exercises in the disputed waters."

"You know very well that the Chinese army is several times stronger than ours. We don't live in 1979 anymore. Compared to that military giant that increases its army spending every year, we are nothing."

"And the Organization of the Southeast Asian Countries have been asked to mediate," Kien argued.

"But China doesn't want that. You can't do business with the Chinese. What are . . . Chinese war ships doing . . . in the South Chinese Sea? . . . Soon . . . every ship . . . check . . . government . . . shutting up . . . agree . . ."

The feeling of dizziness remained, and I found it difficult to speak. Has my vision become blurred?

Kien looked frozen when Ngoc slapped my face. "Show me your tongue! Show me your teeth!"

I tried to follow her orders, but I only partially succeeded.

"Left corner of the mouth down. Probably a stroke. Hospital immediately."

"Which one? . . . suburb . . . evening rush hour . . ."

I registered a few words.

"Thai . . . Ha . . ." I stuttered. "Thai . . . Ha . . . Doctor Kiet . . . Kiet . . . has . . . treated me . . ."

"Phuc. GPS."

Rummaging in the glove compartment.

"Thai Ha."

A device around my arm. Pumping.

"170 over 90. Not much time left."

"5.4 kilometers."

"Siren!"

"Raise your arm," ordered Ngoc. "Raise your arm!"

Impossible to raise the right arm.

Slaps in the face.

"Count to ten!"

"One . . . two . . . six . . ."

Ngoc again, "Faster, driver!"

"Thai Ha . . . church . . . monastery . . . factory . . . already three years . . . fighting . . . praying . . ."

Again slaps to my face.

"Five hundred meters . . ."

"Stop . . . siren off . . . become crazy!"

Body trembling.

"Groups . . . candles . . . praying . . . singing . . . *Song of Peace* . . . Kim Long."

6:00 p.m.

Panting heavily. Left hand clutching the bed rail. Want to sit upright.

"Coming . . . going . . . candles . . . *Song of Peace* . . . Use me . . . instrument . . . your peace."

Ngoc shouting, "Aspirin!"

Mouth open. Water.

"Pill. Swallow. Now!"

Mouth shut. Shirt wet.

"Van Loi . . . Van Loi . . ."

Trying to tap the window.

"Van Loi twice, three times, four times . . . running away . . ."

"Help is coming."

Sliding door opens.

" . . . Stuck . . ."

Siren again.

Left turn.

The GPS's voice said, "Return. Return."

"GPS off!"

Again slapping to my face.

"Show me your tongue! Pinch my hand. Good." Ngoc sighing.

I saw her more sharply again.

"Show me your teeth! Repeat after me: one, two, three."

"One." Panting. "Two . . . three . . ."

Ngoc felt my forehead and took my blood pressure again.

"150 over 80. Phew!" Sigh of relief.

"The storm has subsided."

Kien loosened his tie. His shirt was soaking wet.

"Breathe calmly, breathe calmly."

Ngoc put her hand on my forehead.

The sweat in my head was slowly disappearing. Only the headache remained.

"Acute danger has passed. The blood clot was dissolved by the aspirin. We better get out of this traffic jam and continue to our final destination. Is there a doctor in the camp?"

Kien nodded. "To the camp Nam Ha," he ordered.

"We have to make a U-turn then," Phuc said after he had programmed the GPS again.

"Turn back then, you stupid idiots."

The driver switched on the siren for a brief moment, and Phuc got out of the car to direct the driver to make a 360-degree turn in the congested traffic. Very slowly we drove through one of the main thoroughfares to the other side of town. I saw the Temple of Literature, Vietnam's oldest building that is dedicated to the Chinese philosopher Confucius. "For centuries this was the intellectual center of Vietnam," I thought to myself. "Today, it is turned into a tourist attraction, because this regime hardly counts any intellectuals. All highly educated South Vietnamese I know and who have survived the re-education camps have emigrated."

Further down amidst a large park stands the mausoleum of Ho Chi Minh. The embalmed body of the man is laid out there. I shook my head. What a horrible monstrosity is plumped down here for an ordinary villain in Soviet style. I was about to say just that when Nurse Ngoc, who apparently could read my mind, called me to order.

"You're not going to talk about Ho Chi Minh again," she warned me sternly.

"I thank you for your decisive action, my guardian angel," I whispered. "Without you, I probably wouldn't have survived."

The woman blushed. "I'm glad you realize that you've crawled through the eye of a needle," she agreed. "You might well be paralyzed or in a coma now."

While driving out of the capital, it had become pitch black outside.

"I'm really hungry," Ngoc sighed.

After receiving the imprimatur of the Lieutenant Colonel, she took the wicker basket with supplies.

"Is that all?" She was disappointed. "There are only six sandwiches left. And there was a dessert for everyone. Only two desserts left. And where are the drinks?"

Accusing glances turned in the direction of the driver, who was just gazing at the road.

The man apologized. "You ate in the restaurant. I thought they were for me."

"You knew very well that this would be our dinner," Kien said angrily. "The camp of Nam Ha is still at least two hours away. And it's likely that when we get there the kitchen will have already closed. So we have to ration what we have. Everyone gets the same amount." He turned to the driver: "You've had your share already."

"But I'm hungry." He cried.

"Give him my share," I said. "I have suffered more years from hunger than I can count on my fingers and toes. I'll survive this until tomorrow morning."

Ngoc protested. "If anyone should eat, it's you. It is medically irresponsible to fast now. After all we've been through, won't you listen to what I say?"

The driver pushed on the accelerator and made a risky overtaking maneuver. The tension in the ambulance mounted rapidly.

"Let's not fight over a little food," I intervened. "You're angry with the driver but this good man had to fast while we were in the restaurant. He must take us safely to the camp, and we still have a long way ahead through the jungle. Let's search for a solution."

"The further we drive away from Hanoi, the smaller the probability of finding food," Kien grumbled. "I've done this route hundreds of times."

"There is still a light over there," I pointed out.

"Stop, driver," ordered the Lieutenant Colonel immediately.

"Phuc, go and have a look."

"There's damn food in abundance," he came back beaming.

"You'll be in deep trouble if you're bullshitting me now," Kien warned him with his finger in the air. But to the Lieutenant Colonel's surprise, there was a bakery behind the facade of a simple house."

"You're lucky," said the baker. "Someone didn't pick up his order."

Loaded with two bags of sandwiches and some bottles of milk, Kien and Phuc got back into the ambulance.

"Come on, drive!" Kien ordered the driver. He let out a deep sigh. "This journey will still come to a good end."

The mood was completely reversed. Everyone ate the bread and cheese with relish.

"A glass of fresh milk will taste good," Ngoc beamed.

"Thanks for the tip," Kien said.

"Miracles happen when you trust each other," I responded. "I intuitively felt that there was more going on in that house. And thanks to the trust of the Lieutenant Colonel, we stopped the car. There are no small things in life. If we hadn't stopped, we would still be arguing about some sandwiches. Our society . . ."

"Calm down, you!" Ngoc warned. "And don't get excited. Otherwise, your blood pressure will go up again because you're probably going to criticize the Communists again."

"Don't worry. I'll make my point calmly. What our society needs is trust. But the foundation of the Communist ideology is distrust. And that only generates envy and hatred."

We arrived at the gate of the military area where the concentration camp Nam Ha is situated.

"Transport of a prisoner," reported Kien who opened the door. He recognized some colleagues. They greeted each other warmly.

"Why so late?" asked one of them.

"The trip was an obstacle course," he sighed. "But now we're almost there."

In theory, a thorough inspection must be carried out, but at this late hour, the guards were not in the mood. They shone their flashlight into the car and let us through.

"The rainy season has only just ended, Kien," warned one of them. "The track in the valley is heavily damaged. Drive carefully."

"We always do," winked the Lieutenant Colonel.

But after a few hundred meters the torture of the outward journey came to my mind again. We drove into a pothole. I almost fell out of my bed.

"Slowly, driver!" commanded Kien.

"Do you want me to strap you down?" Ngoc asked. "Those belts will absorb the worst shocks."

I nodded.

The driver steered the ambulance along the potholes and puddles. When Ngoc almost fell off her seat, she grabbed the bed with both hands. Kien put his outstretched legs against my bed for support, but when the chassis touched the ground he got hurt. He groaned in pain, "More slowly, driver!"

I tried to relax by praying, but all these bumps prevented me from focusing. I felt pain everywhere. With my left hand, I held on more tightly to the belts to absorb the shocks, but I gradually lost my grip and my body slid to and fro.

"Stop," I said imploringly. "I can't stand it anymore."

Kien ordered the driver to stop. He also changed his position.

Ngoc flopped down on her seat. "I've never experienced anything like this."

When the driver wanted to restart, the tires started to slip.

"Damn it, now this!" Kien grumbled. He beat the door with his fist.

"Now what?" Ngoc asked.

"What do you think? Phuc, and you, too, help with pushing."

"That's not a job for a nurse!"

"That's an order!"

"That's a man's job."

"You may still need to lend a hand."

"I have a better idea," Ngoc argued. "I'll take the wheel. The driver weighs more than I do."

"Never!" the driver exclaimed. "My car. I drive."

Ngoc looked Kien straight in the eye. "Indeed," he said.

But the driver yelled, "I drive," and he grasped the steering wheel with both hands.

Kien sourly looked at Ngoc as his polished uniform shoes sank firmly into the mud.

"Come on, Phuc!" he ordered.

Reluctantly, Phuc followed his example. Both pushed with all their might and the tires eventually regained their grip. Ngoc breathed a sigh of relief.

"Continue to drive slowly," commanded Kien.

Cursing, Phuc and Kien got back in the car. They were covered in mud.

"The worst is behind us," Kien sighed as the road started to go uphill.

Half an hour later, we began to see the distant lights of the camp fence.

When the driver honked, two guards opened the gate.

In the courtyard, loudspeakers blared out communist militant songs. This happened at the end of each re-education session.

"Is that our welcome?" I grinned. "Wishing someone who is long dead a life of 10,000 years? For years now, I've known in my heart that nobody believes that crap anymore. This playlist should be updated."

The smiling Deputy Director walked towards us. I ignore that cynical man with whom I've argued for years.

"A small delay?" His face then contorted when water began to run out of the opened car door and when Kien then Phuc get out, both covered in mud.

"Next year, we will pave the bad stretch of road in the valley."

"I heard that promise in the late 1980s when I first came here," I said.

The man ignored me. "You can refresh yourself in the residential block."

Kien wanted to tell me something, but in the presence of the Deputy Director, he couldn't get the words out of his mouth. "I expect your report on the journey tomorrow," the Deputy Director said.

"Of course," replied Kien, who looked back and slowly left.

"Thank you," said Phuc, waving at me. I looked up in surprise.

"Who are you thanking?" the Deputy Director asked.

"Nurse Ngoc," Phuc confidently replied. "Good nurse." He stuck up his thumb. Again I saw the oily smile on his face. The nurse was embarrassed by the unexpected compliment, and I too had to smile.

Meanwhile, Ngoc untied my belts, but I could barely move. With great effort, I sat up straight. "Don't stand there grinning, get a wheelchair," she ordered the Deputy Director. "Don't you see that the Reverend can't stand on his legs."

Even with Ngoc's help, getting out of the ambulance required lots of effort.

A guard is quick to bring us a wheelchair.

Ngoc clicked open the footrests to place my feet on, and it took a while for me to catch my breath. "The Evangelist John . . . was right, 'When you're old, . . . somebody else will put a belt around you and take you where you would rather not go.' I've become an old man."

I looked around. "Another five years," I sighed.

Will my decrepit body survive this ordeal? To want to but to be unable to is one of the worst psychological ordeals. Will I ever leave this place of damnation? Will I ever breathe in the air of freedom again? I can only pray, hope, and above all trust that my beloved country will be freed of communism.

8

9:00 p.m.

"This may sound strange to your ears, but this feels like a homecoming," I told the nurse when I stepped through the second gate. The armed guards opened and closed the gate without uttering a word.

Things had hardly changed since I arrived here for the first time a quarter of a century ago. I see in the twilight the foot of a lush hillside with its tropical flora and fauna. The camp is still divided into zones separated by high walls. Over there, the sleeping barracks. Each of them had two dormitories with sixty wooden bunk beds, but sometimes ninety to one hundred prisoners slept there. The square in front served as a gathering point. The bathing facilities where we bathed every Sunday were next to the water tower. We, the prisoners, wore a dark blue prison uniform with the word "Re-education" printed on it.

My mind goes back to when I first came to Nam Ha.

"What I have experienced here," I mused. Although, in the late 1980s, the relocation was not so bad. I had expected worse because, as a general rule, living conditions were harsher the further one went north. Compared to Thanh Cam, the older camp guards did not usually act so brutally. Moreover, physical punishments were proportionate to the offenses; the only exception was the Deputy Director.

"Why don't you bow for me with your eyes to the ground?" the Deputy Director shouted at me. "You know the rules!"

"I have pain in my back."

He grinned and wanted to make an example to the other prisoners. "You're forbidden from writing a letter this moth or receiving a food parcel from your family."

"Do you want to grab it?"

"Guards, take him away!" he reacted furiously. "Solitary confinement in an isolation cell with his feet shackled."

Six months later I was very angry. "The prison guards shouldn't steal food from one of the weakest inmates. Certainly now I'll fight against that unjust act, because they don't handle the criminal gangs in the same way."

My friend, the poet Nguyen Chi Thien, tried to convince me. "Your protests don't make sense."

"But many will support my action," I answered self-secured.

"You've been in camps for the past nine years and you should, in principle, regain your freedom next year. You know very well that one pretext is sufficient to prolong your internment. Is that what you want?"

"Do I have to agree with what's going on here?"

Thien felt my hesitation and argued, "The Camp Director will be pleased if you continue your actions. Don't fall into that trap! Don't gamble your future. Once outside these four walls, you'll probably be under house arrest, but at least you'll have more freedom than you do now. Many opponents of the regime will receive you with open arms. Who's so eloquent? Who has such a sharp pen? Which Vietnamese dissident is at the top of the list of all international human rights organizations? You can do much more outside the prison walls than in this well of oblivion."

"Maybe you're right."

"I'm right."

"But . . . who writes such memorable poems? You are the greatest poetic talent of your generation."

Nguyen Chi Thien reacted resigned, "Since I delivered a collection of four hundred poems to the British Embassy in '79, I've spent twelve years behind these bars here. First in the "Hanoi Hilton," where the American prisoners of war were imprisoned during the war, and now here."

"Your poems give me a lot of strength. I hope when I'm not here anymore, you'll continue to find inspiration and sheets of paper to write your poems on."

"Don't worry. All the poems I've written over here are etched in my memory. Nobody can delete them."

"I'm so pleased with your newest poem *My Verses*. I was privileged to witness how that was created. Are you going to revise your latest version?"

"As I've told you, this is the final version," he smiled.

"You depict the atmosphere in the camp so accurately and in very simple words."

"Once I'm free I'll compose a new collection of poems. I've already found a name for the cover: *Flowers from Hell*."

"That's great!"

In March 2010, in the Archdiocese of Hue, Phan Van Loi secretly gave me a copy of that book. He had hidden it under his cassock, and I hid it for months under the mattress of my bed. But one day the Lieutenant Colonel Kien discovered it.

"What are you reading?" he shouted.

"That's not your business."

The Lieutenant Colonel Kien grabbed the book out of my hands and shouted: "*Flowers from Hell* by Nguyen Chi Thien! That wasn't in your luggage when you arrived here. Where did it come from? How did you get it?"

"A miracle," I smiled.

9:00 p.m.

The Lieutenant Colonel was furious.

"Don't you believe in miracles?" I challenged him. "That's a pity. But I don't need that book any more. You can confiscate it. I know the most important poems by heart." I raised my voice:

> My verses are in fact no verses
> They are simply Life's sobbings
> Dark prison cells opening and shutting
> The dry cough of two caving in lungs
> The sound of earth coming down to bury dreams
> The exhumation sound of hoes bringing up memories
> The chattering of teeth in cold and misery
> The aimless contractions of an empty stomach
> The hopeless beat of a dying heart
> Impotence's voice in the midst of collapsing earth
> All the sounds of a life not deserving half its name
> Or even the name of death:
> No verses are they!

"Can we stop for a moment?" I beg Nurse Ngoc. "This trip in the wheelchair is really a torture. My whole body is suffering."

"Sorry if I'm walking too fast. We'll wait for a while."

"You know," I said as I was looking round, "So many memories are coming to my mind."

"Good or bad memories?

"What do you think?"

"Sorry. This is my first visit to a camp. This is indeed a frightening place. Are you treated well here? The workings must be controlled by the government, aren't they?"

I looked surprised. "Did you say 'control'? Yes, there was once control when I was staying here. In 1988, due to persistent reports of torture and ill treatment in the Vietnamese camps, twenty representatives of international human rights organizations were allowed to visit the camp. In this way, the government wanted to show that the prisoners were very well treated."

"What happened?"

"Before their visit, the living spaces were embellished and the camp library got new books and current magazines. The sick were moved to nearby hospitals and half of the prisoners went out to work, creating the impression that the camp was not overcrowded. My name was on top of the list of persons who would have to leave the camp for that one day. The camp management knew that I would speak up. Poet Nguyen Chi Thien was allowed to stay. 'Anyway, you seized the opportunity to ask a question,' I told him in the evening. 'The observers who visited the workshops were warned not to talk to the prisoners. When a man sought eye contact and I put up my hand in the air, I immediately felt a gun barrel in my back. I was, after all, standing in the last row.' 'And?' I asked. 'It would be a pity if a work accident would happen today,' a guard whispered in my ear. When I felt a second rifle barrel, I lowered my arm."

"Did no one ask questions?"

"Yes, but the prison officers replied. And at the end, a ceremony was conducted on the square where on the occasion of the *Tet* festival one hundred prisoners were given amnesty."

I shook my head. "I don't understand why international human rights organizations participate in such charades. In 1983, Amnesty International adopted me as a prisoner of conscience. But do they defend my rights? They know that I'm here."

Nurse Ngoc was impressed by the surroundings. "Don't you often feel lonely here?"

"What do you think? You get never used to it. Certainly not in the isolation cells."

"Can you receive visitors over here?

I smiled, but in a bitter way. During the last decade I longed for more frequent visits of my sister Tri Hieu the longer I stayed here. I used to reminisce for months after her visit, but now I missed her more and more. She was my second mother. She stood by my side during my priestly ordination; she helped me with moving to various parishes; and she visited me as often as possible in the camps. She spent her last savings on parcels for me, and she brought the maximum that she was allowed to bring with her. I never heard her complain about money or about the day's journey to the camp and back. After my conviction in 2007, I had to wait one and a half years for her first visit here.

"How I've longed for this moment. Since my arrest, there hasn't been an hour that I haven't thought of you!" I gave her a big hug.

"I wasn't allowed to come earlier."

"What would I do without you?"

"Let me have a good look at you." My sister looked me over like mother used to. "You look good."

"What's good?" I sighed. I looked at my head guard, Major Kien, who is obliged to follow our conversation. "They don't even give me pen and paper. And I'm still in solitary confinement. Do not think that I pled guilty because I'm wearing this magnificent black and white striped prison uniform. I wasn't given a choice. Otherwise the Deputy Director would have refused your visit. The mere thought that I wouldn't see you would have driven me mad."

"Can you more or less fill your days?"

"I read the magazine *Right* that you sent me and also the Communist Party's newspaper *Nhan Dan*. But I doubt that I am aware of the real situation in the country. A couple of months ago, we were even allowed to watch TV for the first time when the regime celebrated one of its greatest triumphs. Imagine, President Nguyen Minh Triet visiting George W. Bush in the White House in Washington. The state television also showed images of the interview with the President on CNN, but without the sound. I don't know what was being said. But I saw, in a flash in the background, a photo of my recent conviction whereby I was literally gagged."

I looked back. Major Kien is taking a bag of coffee.

"Do you know more?" I whispered.

"Phan Van Loi, who else, gave me a tape of that conversation," Thi Hieu spoke into my ear. "He had downloaded it from the Internet."

"He's such a wonderful guy! What did Triet say?"

"That you're in prison because of violating the law, and not for religious reasons."

"He's at his best when he's lying!"

"Shh. Quiet! When they showed him the picture where you were gagged, he said, 'That person has made a mistake. This is against our policies.'"

"The hypocrite! Since the Communist takeover, I've been gagged for the past 36 years."

"Triet also denied that Vietnam has prisoners of conscience."

"How dare he! I will continue to fight until the authorities recognize that Vietnam has prisoners of conscience."

"Don't get upset like that. It's not good for your health." Thi Hieu looked worried. "But what's wrong? You're so nervous." She looked at me, straight in my eyes.

I saw the Major chatting with a colleague.

"I don't know. During the last *Tet* holiday I wept the whole time."

"Why?"

"Remember how we used to be with the whole family at home worshipping at the tablets of our ancestors? Who will remember me when I die here in this dungeon? Will there be a tablet of me at the family altar?"

Overcome with emotion, I started to cry.

"What are you talking about, my little brother? How could we ever forget you?" she whispered. "You have done more good in your life than this whole gang of corrupt Communists. In a free Vietnam, your name will be written in golden letters."

She put my head on her lap like mother used to do. "I hope you will see that day. That's what I pray for every day."

With her magic hands, she soothed me of all the frustrations that had accumulated.

"Thank you for giving me what I asked for each time in my letters," I said wiping away the last traces of tears. "Unfortunately, I don't get everything you send me. I know, for example, that the Bible arrived, but the Deputy Director refuses to give it to me because he likes to annoy me." I shook my head and suddenly I burst out laughing.

"What's so funny about that?"

"You know, you're the second person to visit me recently."

"Who?" asked Hieu surprised.

"Last month, to my surprise, the former director of the Major Seminary of Hue visited me. He and I were sentenced for the first time in 1977. To his amazement, he was welcomed with all honors because the Camp Director was convinced he was a Municipal Councilor. Of course, the man played along with the Director, with the result that I was allowed to keep the sacramental wine and the little box of wafers that he had with him."

Without seeing him, Major Kien stood at our table again and intervened. "No more criticizing or the conversation is over. By the way, your visiting time is up in five minutes."

"Send your letters to 'Mr. Nguyen Van Ly' and not to 'Reverend Father Nguyen Van Ly.' The Vietnamese postal service doesn't forward letters to prisons with the word priest in the address because officially, there are no priests in prisons." Looking straight at the Major, I added cynically, "That happens in application of the religious freedom that our Constitution guarantees."

"I will," said Hieu who could hardly suppress a smile. "And here's your package with food and reading material."

Kien took delivery. "After checking it, I will deliver the items that you are allowed to receive to your cell. Sign this receipt."

I signed as "Reverend Nguyen Van Ly, prisoner of conscience."

Hieu nodded approvingly, "You haven't changed." She gave me a kiss.

"Welcome back!" A guard I've gotten to know through the years opens the door of the block with the isolation cells. We understand each other without words. This is necessary, because if someone should notice that our relationship is friendly, the guard would automatically be transferred.

"Sorry, it's not my fault that you've ended up here again instead of in the barracks," he whispers. "The Deputy Director, you know."

"I don't blame you at all. How many years have we known each other?"

"I entered the service on December 1, 1989."

"In a few years, you will celebrate your silver jubilee! Will I receive an invitation as a loyal customer?"

The man shook his head.

"Well, without us, you'd be out of work," I teased him.

"Hey, come with me to the Reverend's cell."

Guards must always work in pairs. But I have no complaints about this guy either. Both are among the most jovial guards in the camp. I can't say the same about most of the other specimens that haunt these premises.

"I made sure that no one else was put in here since your departure eighteen months ago. This is, after all, your cell."

"I didn't know I had so many privileges!"

While Ngoc pushed my wheelchair, I was welcomed by my fellow prisoners. I heard some familiar voices because in a place where things seldom happen, news spreads like wildfire.

"Bad weeds grow quickly," I heard behind me.

"Does the Deputy Director know that you're back?"

"We expected you six months ago," my neighbor said. "It's very quiet here. Hopefully, that will change now."

When the guard opened the cell door and switched on the light, I concluded that nothing had changed. Four bare walls, a bed, a chair, a small table, and a small window near the ceiling. You can't take more than three steps, but that's also all I'm physically able to do. And the floor is still shiny. It was laid there a few years ago to impress foreign visitors, but I'm still waiting for the first foreign visitor. It was in this cell that my health problems started. In late 2008, my high blood pressure caused signs of temporary paralysis.

9:00 p.m.

"He's a comedian," the Deputy Director said to the camp doctor. Both were standing outside my cell. "He doesn't need any treatment."

After my first stroke in May 2009, the camp doctor refused treatment again. "Here's some medicine to stem the blood flow from your head wound after you've fallen down. That'll be enough."

"Is that all?" I protested. "What if this happens again? I need a medical treatment."

"Are you the doctor or am I?" he shouted. "I decide on medical affairs."

"What happened?" I asked when I woke up in my cell one day in September 2009.

"You've suffered a second stroke," answered the doctor. "You're partially paralyzed on the right side of your body. Here's your medication."

"That's very kind," I reacted with vitriol. "Will you inform my sister?"

"I'll ask your head guard."

Furiously, my sister entered the camp. "Why am I only informed now?" she asked Major Kien. "My brother had a stroke a month ago! This won't happen again." She took a piece of paper. "Here are two telephone numbers. Call me and the Archbishop of Hue immediately if my brother's health deteriorates further."

Later in November 2009, the camp doctor received a panicked phone call from a guard. "Prisoner Van Ly is lying on the ground of his cell. He's unconscious."

"Call an ambulance," reacted the man stoically. "I'm coming."

After examination the camp doctor concluded, "He has had a third stroke. Transfer him to the prison hospital."

In Hanoi, five policemen permanently guarded me. Doctor Kiet gave my file and the X-rays a thorough examination. "Two arteries in your neck are blocked and, due to a one-inch tumor in the left part of your brain, the right side of your body is paralyzed."

"What has to happen next," I inquired.

The man frowned and left the room.

"Pack your things," Lieutenant Colonel Kien ordered one month later.

"Why? Am I being transferred to the camp again?" I reacted disconcertedly. "My health has barely improved. I want to speak Doctor Kiet."

"Your situation is under control now," smiled the doctor. "There'll be no problem returning to your cell. You can take your adapted medication with you."

I was flabbergasted when I heard on the radio in the ambulance that Pope Benedict XVI had granted an audience to President Nguyen Minh Triet in Rome.

"That's no coincidence, but another provocation of the Government in an attempt to break me mentally," I reacted on a bitter tone. "But they won't succeed!"

But I was even more stunned by the second item on the news: "The trade relations of Vietnam with the United States and Europe are improving further."

"If Westerners can benefit from economic growth, they turn a deaf ear when human rights are discussed," I told Kien.

A few months later, in January 2010, the camp doctor entered my cell; he was angry.

"Now what are you doing?"

"Yesterday I began a hunger strike in order to unite me in prayer with the parishioners of Dong Chiem," I confidently answered. "They had planted a cross on a piece of church land seized by the authorities. It was removed by the authorities, but immediately a new cross was erected."

"This is medically irresponsible and not my responsibility. You dig your own grave!

To my surprise Kien entered my cell on March 5, 2010.

"Pack your things," he ordered.

"What's happening here? First of all my congratulations! I just heard that you've been promoted to Lieutenant Colonel."

"Thank you. It's my duty to communicate a decision of the People's Court." The man stood straight and read on a solemn tone: 'For humanitarian reasons, the Court has decided to move you to the retirement home for priests of the Archdiocese of Hue for twelve months.'"

I was so taken aback that the contents of the letter completely escaped me. "Can you read this again?" I stuttered.

Kien resumed his solemn attitude and read the letter for the second time.

An ambulance was waiting in the courtyard.

Upon arrival in Hue, I got an enthusiastic welcome from the Auxiliary Bishop of the Archdiocese of Hue, Francis Le Van Hong, and some colleagues led by my trusted comrade in arms, Phan Van Loi.

"Do you have an explanation for what is happening here?"

"Human rights organizations, including Amnesty International and Human Rights Watch, have been working for years towards your release. Yet it was the 7th Australian Vietnamese Dialogue on Human Rights last week that tipped the balance."

"Not again!" I exclaimed. On the table in my cell, I saw the quarterly self-assessment form that I must complete. "Is that stupid procedure going to start again?"

"The Deputy Director gave us the form this morning," said the guard. "This is a directive from the Ministry. You'd better comply, otherwise . . ."

"Nurse Ngoc, can you do me a favor? Tear up this form and give it back."

I turn to the guards. "Please tell the Deputy Director that I'm unable to write because of my paralysis, but I'd be happy to comply with the administrative regulations during a personal conversation with him."

Before the incredulous eyes of the guards, Ngoc tore up the form into a hundred pieces. "And now, please leave us alone! I'm going to put the Reverend to bed."

Ngoc tucked me in.

"Thank you for your care," I said, sighing deeply. Would you be so kind as to take my breviary out of my bag?"

I gave her the cross that I had gotten from the Bahnar woman we met during our journey. She was moved.

"You've earned this, because you are a good person."

The guards looked surprised when Ngoc gave me a hug and got up with a broad smile.

"Tell the camp doctor to come as soon as possible. During the trip, the Reverend almost suffered a stroke again, and he should be monitored medically. And at least give him an aspirin every day."

"Good night!" With a firm stride she walked away.

The door slammed shut. Finally, some rest. The piece of paper in my breviary was still stuck at Chapter 40 of the Book of Isaiah. I read those haunting verses once more:

> Speak tenderly to Jerusalem, and proclaim to her
> That her hard service has been completed.

The end of the exile; it is very close. I could see this with my own eyes today. This is also the real Advent. Although all my limbs ache, I hardly feel the pain because of the sense of satisfaction that fills me. The changing of the guard is assured. Isn't this a wonderful time to bow out? I feel ready for the big crossing. For the first time since my time in the seminary, I don't write down a thought in preparation for tomorrow's meditation. Isn't everything completed?

I glide into a deep sleep.

9:00 p.m.

I wake up with a start. Someone is knocking on my door. The light in my cell is still switched on. I hear the rattling of keys. The door swings open. I'm still half asleep when Kien appears before me with his puffy cheeks and wearing a freshly ironed uniform. He takes off his cap; there are still traces of mud on the Coat of Arms of Vietnam.

"What do you want at this hour of the night? Don't you want me to rest?"

"I want to . . ." The man seems lost.

"You don't have to wait," he tells the guards. "I'll call you when I'm ready. I still have to write a report. I will have hand it over to the Director tomorrow."

The guards leave and the door is closed.

Kien is acting strangely. He looks like a beaten dog.

"What's wrong?"

Without a word he gives me the crumpled package containing the book about the demonstration in Vinh.

"It's better like that. I feel that this is dear to you. If I make a report, the police will also interrogate the woman in Vinh. And who knows what other consequences this will have."

I am pleasantly surprised. "Thank you very much." With great effort I put my back against the wall, because all my muscles ache.

There is a silence.

The Lieutenant Colonel wants to tell me something but cannot find the words.

I decided to break the ice, because there's also something on my mind. "Today, I've been pretty hard on you," I confess. "Please accept my apologies. But it is stronger than myself. I am influenced by my perpetual struggle for what is dearest to me on earth—freedom. The grooves on my arms and legs have become deeper with the years. They have eventually reached my bones. When I try to smooth out my wrinkles, they return automatically. My body and my struggles are tethered. I will fight until my last breath, even if no one hears me. It is essentially you who has borne the brunt, because you represent the regime that keeps everyone under thumb in this country."

Kien sits on the edge of my bedstead and shakes his head. He lets out a deep sigh. "Not you. It is I who must apologize. Now I can finally tell you what bothers me. I couldn't do that in Hue, because your room, and even the kitchen, was bugged, and during our afternoon walks, Phuc always accompanied me. For seven years, I've been treating you according to the book of rules. A few times I asked to be transferred because of your eternal grumbling, and your pedantry sometimes made me despair. My request was refused each time. None of my colleagues wanted my job. I had no choice. I had to stay on."

"How is that possible?"

"When I was eighteen, I trained at the Institute of Marxist-Leninist Studies in Hanoi, you know, the elite school of the party. Anyone who is admitted there will have a brilliant career. But because of a student prank that went wrong and for which others blamed me, I was sent away. Yes, I got a second chance. But I had to start over again at the bottom. Since then, a sword of Damocles has been hanging over my head. The slightest misstep would be fatal to me, and I can never say no. Since my promotion, I have focused on Zen meditation. That has made me a calmer person, but today my bucket has overflowed. I'm ashamed . . . to have been for twenty years . . . an instrument . . . that sustains this corrupt and immoral regime."

He can't stop the flood of tears.

"I'm desperate. Since our arrival here, I've been playing with the idea of resigning. I'm unable to pretend any longer."

For a moment I don't know how to react. Finally, I say, "Don't do that! You know better than anyone that they will destroy you. Or do you prefer to work as a sweeper or in a coffee plantation?"

"Maybe I'll emigrate."

"Would you desert your sick wife and your handicapped daughter?"

"I want out of here! Out! Out! Out!"

"Where do you want to go?"

"I thought of Russia."

"Do you speak Russian?"

Silence.

Recently, many Vietnamese have entered Russia illegally.

"For a lot of money, a people trafficker will take you to Moscow. And then what? In Russia, there are hardly any charitable institutions. I once heard of a shelter run by a certain Alexandr, a man who spent many years in the concentration camps. But will you find him? And would he be able to help you? If you're not immediately arrested by the police, you will end up in the illegal labor market. You will be exploited, and you'll have to work in difficult conditions for a pittance. The Russian mafia is worse than the Vietnamese one. And now that Putin's party has won last Sunday's elections, he'll be President again in March next year. As a full-blooded nationalist, Putin hates all illegal immigrants. You would certainly be sent back. With a little luck, you'd find yourself in the cell next to mine."

Kien is a broken man.

"What I don't understand is your desperation, while only a couple of hours ago you were confidently defending the regime that you despise."

"I had no choice. I don't know Nurse Ngoc, but the other people in the ambulance are spies. The driver can neither read nor write, but each day he reports on what he has seen and heard over the telephone. And Phuc has to send in a report about me every day, as I do about him. Also, the Archbishop's Palace in Hue is full of secret agents. Do you know that?"

"I know. But I have nothing to hide. Everywhere I always say what I think. My body is imprisoned, but my thoughts are free."

"While I walk around freely, my thoughts are burdened by the Communist yoke."

We smile, but the undertone is acerbic.

"And I would like you to remain my Head Guard," I say hesitantly.

The Lieutenant Colonel doesn't believe his ears. "What do you mean? You've scolded me the whole day!" He pauses and looks at me with concern. "Are you afraid?"

I hesitate for a moment, then I nod. "Another five years in this prison. And I have already suffered four strokes. I don't think I'll survive a new Head Guard. In the past, I've met a number of bullies. Each time I was mentally stronger than them, so that they left. But now I lack the strength. I can't make a fist anymore. I have no energy left in me. My body is shattered."

"The do-gooder who thinks of himself," he jokes.

That remark cuts into my heart, but it contains a kernel of truth.

"I'm not naturally like that," I defend myself. "But still, I think . . . it's also the best solution for you."

"Why?"

"I won't mock you anymore. And if you have your sick wife transferred to Hanoi, you can spend every weekend with her. It's now that she needs you most. And during the week that you're off duty, every month both of you can visit your daughter. The real solution to your problems, however, lies in deepening your faith."

"You want me near you to have a better opportunity to convert me?"

"I have only baptized people who asked for it. But the answer to the question you're struggling with is obvious. You grew up in a Buddhist environment, but you've repressed your religious feelings for your career. Without realizing it you've returned to the source that you crave. Commit yourself to the study of Buddhism. Go to the temple in your spare time. Seek advice from Buddhist monks. Religions have, unfortunately, often degenerated into systems of oppression, but religion itself is liberating. 'Stand fast, therefore, in the liberty by which Christ made us free, and do not be entangled again with a yoke of bondage,' writes Paul in Galatians 5:1. It's the same for Buddhism. But you must make the step towards your own liberation, because nobody can make that decision for you."

The dull look in Kien's eyes has disappeared.

"A Catholic priest who advertises Buddhism; that's something I've never experienced."

"The Catholic tradition is in my genes. But if I would have grown up in a Buddhist family, I'd probably be a Buddhist monk now."

"What is the difference between Buddhism and Catholicism?"

"Nguyen Van Thuan, 'my' president of the seminary and one of the most profound thinkers I've ever met, once used a metaphor that gets to the heart of the issue. The principles of Christians, Buddhists, Muslims, Taoists, and Hindus seem, at first sight, totally incompatible, but look more closely, and you'll see that this is not the case at all. After all, we are all climbing the same mountain, albeit along a different edge. Everyone hopes to reach the top to meet a Supreme Being that is infinitely greater than we are. However, regardless of the religion we profess, we are brothers. During our journey on earth, our ascent of the mountain, we are all equal and walk side by side like real brothers."

Kien is petrified.

"Can I have my bag?"

I take Van Loi's CD and give it to him. "In your room, listen to the finale of Beethoven's Ninth Symphony. Only then will you understand everything." I take the booklet and I recite:

> Anger and revenge be forgotten
> Our deadly enemy be forgiven.
> No tears shall he shed
> No remorse shall gnaw at him.

"And here is the refrain:

> Your magic brings together
> What custom has sternly divided.
> All men shall become brothers,
> Wherever your gentle wings hover.

"In composing his symphony, Beethoven was inspired by the "Ode to Joy" from the German philosopher Friedrich von Schiller. The text is also in the booklet. Look, read the last lines."

His voice echoes in my cell:

Be embraced, millions!
This kiss to the entire world!
Brothers, above the starry canopy
A loving Father must reside.
Do you fall down, you millions?
Do you sense the Creator, world?
Seek him above the starry canopy!
Above the stars, he must live!

"I know Beethoven by name only, but I've never heard of Schiller," he says while looking at the text in amazement.

"I know of no more powerful synthesis reflecting the essence of life. This is the text of the European anthem," I said yawning. "It should be the anthem of the United Nations, the G20, and the world. If everyone would carry a piece of that dream, the world would look different . . . But I'm going to bed now. I'm exhausted."

Kien helps me lie down. "Thank you for your wisdom, your insight, and your advice. I will take that to heart. And this evening, I'll listen to the CD."

He stood up and looked back. "I think I'll stay here, my brother."

I smiled and I fell into a deep sleep.

Kien tapped on the door with his keys.

Moments later, the guards opened it. "Is your report ready?"

Kien turned off the light, looked behind him one last time, and then showed them the CD. "Do you know that this is the most important report that has ever been written?"

www.ingramcontent.com/pod-product-compliance
Lightning Source LLC
LaVergne TN
LVHW010932100826
845153LV00001B/11

9781498289542